Grades K–3

SCIENCE & STORIES

Integrating Science and Literature

Grades K–3

SCIENCE & STORIES

Integrating Science and Literature

Hilarie N. Staton

Tara McCarthy

Science Advisor: Julie Kane Brinkmann

Good Year Books

Good Year Books

are available for most basic curriculum subjects plus many enrichment areas. For more Good Year Books, contact your local bookseller or educational dealer. For a complete catalog with information about other Good Year Books, please contact:

Good Year Books
P.O. Box 91858
Tucson, AZ 85752-1858
www.goodyearbooks.com

Book design by Street Level Studio.
Copyright © 1994 Hilarie N. Staton and Tara McCarthy.
All Rights Reserved.
Printed in the United States of America.

ISBN-10 1-59647-082-8
ISBN-13 978-1-59647-082-8
Previous ISBN 0-675-56083-0

10 11 12 13 14 - ML - 07 06 05

Only portions of this book intended for classroom use may be reproduced without permission in writing from the publisher.

Table of Contents

From *Science & Stories*, Grades K-3, published by GoodYearBooks. Copyright © 1994 Hilarie N. Staton and Tara McCarthy.

7. RESOURCES

From *Science & Stories, Grades K-3*, published by GoodYearBooks. Copyright © 1994 Hilarie N. Staton and Tara McCarthy.

Making Connections

SCIENCE AS A PART OF WHAT YOU'RE ALREADY DOING

The ancient Greeks thought of knowledge as holistic, recognizing that everything was related to everything else. While educational strategy in general is returning to this classic insight, teachers in Grades K–3 have always followed it! We've always known about the overlap between curricular areas. We've known that it's natural to connect math to making a chart or graph in social studies, to flow from a rhyming words exercise in phonics to a great poem we want to share with students and then invite them to act it out or illustrate it.

Nowhere is holistic classroom instruction more practical today than in the areas of literature and science. New science curriculums encourage students to discover meanings and relationships and to find and practice ways of solving problems. New science curriculums stress that the understanding of processes is more important than the abilty to describe products, and that the ability to organize is more important than rote memorization of facts. These emphases are the same ones elementary teachers are already stressing as they use good literature in the classroom. We want our students to focus on the meanings and implications of a story, relate the tale to their own lives, and analyze how story characters solve problems.

Now that making connections between curricular areas is praised and encouraged, teachers no longer have to struggle to fit those mandated 100–125 minutes per week of science instruction into already overloaded schedules. Because they often use similar approaches, science and literature can go hand-in-hand.

KEY COMPONENTS OF YOUR SCIENCE PLAN

Four key components of the science process involve problem solving, obtaining knowledge, understanding the nature of science, and finding relationships among science, technology, and society. Current science curricula suggest that at grade levels K–3, problem-solving takes 50 to 60 percent of your science instruction time; with science knowledge taking about 20 percent; understanding the nature of science about 10 percent; and science/technology/society about 10 percent.

1. DEVELOPING PROBLEM-SOLVING SKILLS

Problem solving in science comprises four recursive, interacting steps: questioning; collecting data; analyzing the data; and explaining. These steps probably sound familiar to you, because you already encourage your students to use them as they enjoy and discuss literature. *Science & Stories* suggests ways to use these familiar steps to set up science activities, building on the science theme and understandings implicit in the literature.

The chart that follows gives some examples of the science and literature connections from this book.

STORY	SCIENCE UNDERSTANDING
The Legend of the Bluebonnet	Water evaporates.

QUESTIONING

What has happened to the land where She-Who-Is-Alone lives?	What will happen to the water in the saucer when we leave it in the sun?

COLLECTING DATA

What happens as the land gets drier? What will happen if no rain comes?	Check the water level in the saucer. What has happened? Check the saucer later. What has happened?

ANALYZING THE DATA

Plants can't grow without water.	Eventually all of the water in the saucer will be gone.

EXPLAINING

The bluebonnets grow and blossom because they finally get water in the form of rain.	Water evaporates into the air. The water comes back in the form of rain.

2. OBTAINING KNOWLEDGE

Through the literature and science activities in this book, your students will find facts to support and supplement the knowledge they're gleaning through whatever basal science textbook program you are using. Students are able to obtain scientific knowledge through the medium of literature. Through literature, science facts take on a relevance and immediacy that helps students remember them and apply them to their own lives.

From *Science & Stories*, Grades K–3, published by GoodYearBooks. Copyright © 1994 Hilarie N. Staton and Tara McCarthy.

3. UNDERSTANDING THE NATURE OF SCIENCE

The nature of science involves its history (its evolution and milestones over time), its philosophy (the assumptions on which it is based and the rules scientists follow), and the interactions of scientists with one another and with technology. Understanding the nature of science becomes increasingly important in the middle grades and in high school.

Science & Stories suggests ways to introduce students in Grades K–3 to this strategy component on the simplest level: to learn through recursive practice some of the rules and procedures scientists follow.

4. FINDING RELATIONSHIPS AMONG SCIENCE, TECHNOLOGY, AND SOCIETY

This strategy component also becomes more important as students proceed into middle school and high school. Your K–3 students, however, begin to investigate the relationships through the stories and through abundant Follow-up Activities in each lesson of *Science & Stories.*

HOW WE CHOSE THE BOOKS IN *SCIENCE & STORIES*

When we started this book, it seemed like an overwhelming task. How could we possibly choose twenty-four books from the thousands of good books out there? It wasn't easy, but we'd like to share some of our thoughts on the process. We hope it will help you choose additional books to use in teaching your science curriculum.

Our first criterion was whether we liked the book. We evaluated each for a clear and interesting story and vivid illustrations. We looked at the classics as well as the newest books. We had to believe the book was good literature before we'd use it. We also tried to make sure the books were easily available, either classics sure to be in the library, or widely available new books.

For our science criteria, we searched through various science curricula to determine what is usually taught at the primary level. We then assessed our favorite books to determine whether they contained science concepts appropriate to the primary grades. Finally, we made sure we could extend the concepts from that story to other areas in the curriculum.

As we looked at the story and science together, we determined whether kids would really get excited about the book and activities. Once we had the book, the concept, and the excitement, writing the activities was easy!

We've included twenty-four books that you can use to teach science. Many more are mentioned in these pages and listed in the bibliography (page 125).

When you choose a book, think about how this story could excite the science interest of students. Be creative, make unusual connections, and invite your students to suggest activities and science concepts from the books. We hope that this is just the beginning of an interesting interchange between the science and literature taught in your class!

From *Science & Stories*, Grades K-3, published by GoodYearBooks. Copyright © 1994 Hilarie N. Staton and Tara McCarthy.

READING-TO-SCIENCE STRATEGIES

READING STRATEGIES

Incorporated into the lessons are opportunities for you to teach reading across the curriculum. You can use the lessons to do the following:

Model thinking processes. Modeling is a monologue that traces your own thinking and decision-making. You think out loud to show students how you think. In the Pre-Reading section of each lesson, for example, you might use the title and cover art as prompts to show students how you remember what you already know, set a purpose for reading, and make predictions. As you introduce *The Story of the Jumping Mouse,* your modeling might proceed like this:

> I like to think about a story before I read it. I'll look at the title and the cover to get an idea of what the story is about. The title here is *The Story of the Jumping Mouse.* So I guess this is a story about a mouse that jumps! I've seen mice before, but never one that jumps. Also, it looks like this mouse lives outdoors instead of in someone's house. I wonder what adventures this jumping mouse has? I'm going to read the book to find out.

Similarly, you can use modeling to show how you can make predictions based on science knowledge you already have, how you draw upon personal experiences as you approach a book, or how you use visual materials to set the stage for reading.

Teach reading strategies. Methods that help students learn to read include the following: (a) Learn key science vocabulary before reading. For example, students can learn the meaning of the word *cell* before reading *The Magic School Bus Inside the Human Body;* (b) Use context to determine word meanings. Many lessons, such as that for *Letting Swift River Go,* contain clues that

suggest the meanings of unfamiliar words; (c) Elaborate on stories by reading the pictures. For an example, see the lesson for *Nightgown of the Sullen Moon;* (d) Use stories to build specific categories of vocabulary. For example, the lesson for *Time of Wonder* suggests building a word bank of sensory words and phrases; (e) Use graphic organizers such as charts, diagrams, or maps to collate information. For example, the lesson for *How to Dig a Hole to the Other Side of the World* suggests that students label a map to trace the story character's adventures; (f) Studying a story to find specific information or to identify problems and solutions. For an example, see the lesson for *Letting Swift River Go* where students use and discuss the five problem-solving steps.

ORAL LANGUAGE SKILLS

All the science and literature connection lessons have strong oral language components.

Listening for specific information, for definitions of terms, and for patterns.
While reading *Hill of Fire,* students listen for the meaning of specific terms having to do with volcanoes. For other examples, see the lessons for *Mandy* and *Witch Hazel.*

Stretching expressive language.
Students have opportunities to do this as they role-play (*Gregory the Terrible Eater*), discuss and categorize words (*I Wonder If I'll See a Whale*), and give directions using spatial concepts (*Katy and the Big Snow*).

Adapting language to different situations.
The lessons provide opportunities to discuss accuracy of statements (*Tiger*); to exchange ideas (*Time of Wonder*); to create stories (*The Nightgown of the Sullen Moon*); to conduct interviews (*Miss Rumphius*); and to listen to and then question a guest speaker (*Bringing the Rain to Kapiti Plain*).

In addition, all the lessons involve students in planning, discussing, and interpreting orally the outcomes and significance of the science activities connected with the literature.

WRITING SKILLS

Each lesson has at least one writing activity, and usually more. Writing activities include the following:

Informal writing assignments.
These include suggestions for keeping journals, taking notes, writing analogies, or creating metaphors.

Writing process assignments.
Students practice pre-writing and organizing skills as they do science activities together, carry out ongoing research activities, or organize data they've collected. The lessons suggest many different forms for writing. Among these are stories, poems, mini-books, interviews, newspaper articles, letters, travel brochures, and descriptions.

Editing and revising activities.
These are usually set in writing conferences in which students talk with one another or with you about their writing goals and about how these goals can be achieved. We also suggest that you use the modeling technique frequently in whole-class writing activities to teach and review how you revise and edit written work.

Whole-language activities. Encourage students to publish and present their written products. The lessons point out ways to incorporate these products as booklets and folders for your reading center or science center; as classroom displays or bulletin boards; or as informal programs for sharing writing with families at home, with classroom visitors, or with other students in your school.

IMPLEMENTING MULTILEVEL INSTRUCTION

"Multilevel instruction" is a new term for what good teachers have been doing all along. They plan interactions and activities that address individual students' strengths and weaknesses and tailor learning objectives to meet individual needs. For example, in the science activity accompanying the lesson for *I Wonder If I'll See a Whale*, teachers know that some students may be able only to categorize birds by their size, most students will be able to add another characteristic, and a few students may be able to develop a multi-characteristic classification system. Yet all students will have practiced the skill of classification.

Here are some suggestions for multilevel adaptations to use with the lessons in this book.

For students who have academic or learning disabilities

1. During reading and oral language activities, ask each question right after students have heard the information. This helps the student who would otherwise have trouble remembering data.

2. For students who have weak receptive language skills, break questions down into smaller segments.

3. If students are slower thinkers and speakers, accept accurate answers that consist of just one word or of a simple sentence.

4. To help ensure that these students come to school with some prior knowledge to contribute to the pre-reading discussion, suggest to their families or to support personnel different activities and materials to use with the students beforehand.

5. Invite slower students to contribute early in the discussion, before the information they bring to class is co-opted by someone else. If students have trouble drawing conclusions and making predictions during these discussions, amplify the context by using more pictures, and help students relate the pictures to their own experience.

6. Play to the students' strengths. If the student is a good listenener, encourage him or her to listen to books on tape or to raise a hand when he or she hears an important idea in a group discussion. If the student is a tactile learner, encourage him or her to manipulate the materials used in the science activities. For visual learners, use graphic organizers (semantic webs, cycle illustrations, charts, story boards) to help clarify concepts.

7. Give poor readers hands-on activities, and invite other students to read the story to them. Or pair poor readers and speakers with patient students who are good readers, so that the former can perfect their reading before taking part in oral reading activities.

8. Use concrete examples to introduce anything new. For example, for Activity Sheet 2, you might need to introduce the concepts *loud* and *soft.* Use your voice to produce examples of the same notes sung softly or loudly.

From *Science & Stories*, Grades K–3, published by GoodYearBooks. Copyright © 1994 Hilarie N. Staton and Tara McCarthy.

9. Accept that some students may not be able to generalize from concrete examples. For example, as students do the science activity for *Bringing the Rain to Kapiti Plain,* some of them may not transfer the information from the book (grass needs rain to grow) to realizing what their plants need to grow. Carefully help them see the parallels. For instance, you can create a visual organizer to show the similarities in the two situations.

10. Consider limiting the vocabulary or concepts you expect some students to master. Focus on one or two of the most important terms (such as magma in *How to Dig a Hole to the Other Side of the World*) and help students master just that term, asking them to define it each time it appears.

For able and gifted students

1. Challenge students who are gifted in one or more areas to use their skills in different ways. Ask them higher-order questions during a science discussion. Invite them to make charts and other graphic organizers that can be used in class discussions. Invite them to share any extra knowledge they have on a particular topic.

2. Call on better students to provide clearer descriptions or definitions or to suggest a new approach to a problem.

3. Occasionally pair a good reader with a poor one. This increases the good reader's self-esteem and can also provide him or her with valuable, mature insights into the learning process.

4. While more able students can use their strengths to help the class as a whole, be careful not to always put them in the tutor or researcher roles. From time to time, create a homogeneous group where able students can challenge one another to go beyond what the class is doing. For example, a group of advanced students can undertake one or more of the activities that extend the science concept rather than limiting themselves to the already mastered problem.

COOPERATIVE LEARNING

In a cooperative learning group, students divide the learning tasks and then share their knowledge. Because students learn by teaching each other, each group member is more likely to learn all the material.

Cooperative learning groups make a strong environment for multi-level modifications. Because these groups are usually heterogeneous, students can be assigned roles that emphasize their strengths. For example, a physically handicapped student may contribute to the group's observation journal, although another student may do the actual writing. If the physically handicapped student uses a computer, he or she may be responsible for creating the final typed product. During the cooperative learning activity for *Katy and the Big Snow,* one student may record the force needed to move each box, while another operates the scale and a third fills the boxes.

Each student is being challenged by activities and interactions that take into account his or her level, strengths, and needs. For a student with a severe behavioral problem, the role might be to praise every other group member at least five times during the group activity.

From *Science & Stories,* Grades K-3, published by GoodYearBooks. Copyright © 1994 Hilarie N. Staton and Tara McCarthy.

There are many ways to organize cooperative learning. Each story in this book has at least one cooperative learning activity. The activities are organized in the ways listed below.

Partner Work. (a) For *Whistle for Willie*, partners work together to make sounds with various objects. (b) For *I Wonder If I'll See a Whale,* partners take turns observing and recording, then use the information to create categories and descriptions. In other activities, partners conduct interviews or write brochures.

Specific Roles That Come Together. (a) For *The Mixed-Up Chameleon*, all members observe, but each has a different role in creating a final product. (b) For *The Nightgown of the Sullen Moon,* students design nightgowns for the moon, then come together to improvise a play, deciding who will be the director, the actors, and the narrator. (c) For *Tiger,* each student is responsible for answering a question developed by the group. Then students gather all their data into a nonfiction book.

Using the Jigsaw Model. In the jigsaw model, each group member chooses a topic related to the whole and gets together with members from other groups who have chosen the same topics. These "expert groups" meet to research, organize, and learn fully about their topic. This done, the students return to their original groups and share their expertise with other group members.

For *Gregory, the Terrible Eater*, for example, expert groups investigate and locate examples of one category of food. Back in their original groups, students teach their teammates about the food category and add it to the group's food pyramid. For *The Magic School Bus Inside the Human Body,* expert groups research organs of the body and then teach their original groups about them.

AUTHENTIC ASSESSMENT

Educators' ideas about assessment have changed considerably. In classrooms where multiple choice tests once held sway, we now find authentic assessment devices such as portfolios, self-assessment scales, and project evaluations. These strategies are particularly encouraged in the new science curriculums.

In this book, opportunities for informal assessment are signalled by this symbol.

The last section of each lesson, Applying the Science Concept, often refers to an Activity Sheet as an assessment device. Some Activity Sheets ask students to apply the science concept to new situations. The Activity Sheet for *The Story of Jumping Mouse,* for example, asks students to apply what they've learned about the senses to their own daily lives. Other Activity Sheets, such as that for *Katy and the Big Snow,* require students to analyze new data on the basis of what they've already learned.

Often you can make assessments of students' progress as they carry out the activity in Building the Science Connection. Related discussions give students a chance to answer questions, make generalizations, and extend the concept.

When cooperative learning groups complete a project, you can carry out a project assessment: (a) Evaluate the entire product or presentation; (b) Evaluate the segment of the project done by

From *Science & Stories*, Grades K-3, published by GoodYearBooks. Copyright © 1994 Hilarie N. Staton and Tara McCarthy.

each member; (c) Ask group members to help you evaluate the processes they used. For example, did group members cooperate and encourage one another? Did they work together to use skills like keeping to the subject? It's sometimes useful to present scales by which students can assess their cooperative work. For example,

	Always	Sometimes	Never
We kept to the subject.			

Many Follow-up Activities give you and your students opportunities to assess the skills of synthesis and elaboration. These across-the-curriculum projects engage students in making further connections in the realms of social studies, math, and the arts.

This book frequently suggests that students keep portfolios throughout a lesson. The portfolios can be used as assessment devices to show how cogently the students have brought together the science and literature connections and how they have connected overarching concepts to other curriculum areas. As you know, portfolio assessment is a cooperative procedure between teacher and student. Get the students to tell you their goals, arrange their portfolios to reflect their goals, fill in steps they think may be missing, and evaluate their own work.

CHARTING AND PLANNING THE SCIENCE CONNECTIONS

The chart on the next page is designed as a quick reference tool with which you can do the following: (a) Find a science understanding that fits well with literature you've chosen for your students; (b) Find a piece of literature that you can use to introduce a science understanding or skill you want your students to develop; (c) Get an overview of the major investigation in each lesson, so that you can spot the ones that are done indoors or outdoors, that are applicable to seasons and weather in your area, or that might, as in the case of field trips, require assistance from parents or other community resource persons; (d) Locate activities in other curriculum areas, such as art, social studies, or health, that you can link to literature or science.

On the chart, the book titles appear in the sequence of the lessons in this book. The sequence was devised (a) to present major themes at increasing levels of complexity; (b) to allow for recursive learning. In recursive learning, students come back to a major theme, such as systems and interactions, from a different angle and with a richer background gleaned from exploring other themes.

This sequence isn't set in stone, however, nor is it necessary to use all the suggested books. Pick and choose from the literature according to your students' reading levels and interests. If you're experimenting with fitting science instruction into a theme-based curriculum, with themes such as Families, Inventions, or Myths and Legends, you might want to choose from the chart some literature that fits into those themes. Turn to the first pages of each lesson for a Story Summary to guide you. For example, *Witch Hazel* and *Hill of Fire* deal in one way or another with family relationships. *The Nightgown on the Sullen Moon*, *How to Dig a Hole to the Other Side of the World*, and *Alexander and the Wind-up Mouse* are naturals for a Make-believe and Reality theme.

Finally, use the chart in conjunction with the Bibliography on pages 125–129. There you'll find suggestions for literature to use in addition to or as replacements for the titles listed on the chart.

From *Science & Stories*, Grades K–3, published by GoodYearBooks. Copyright © 1994 Hilarie N. Staton and Tara McCarthy.

CHART OF LITERATURE-SCIENCE CONNECTIONS

Literature	Major Theme	Science Concept	Investigations	Curricular Links
1. *Witch Hazel* pp. 1–5	patterns of change	Plants go through stages of development.	patterns of plant growth	oral language, writing, math, music, art
2. *Whistle for Willie* pp. 6–9	methods of observation	Sound moves in all directions.	noting different sounds	oral language, writing, social studies
3. *Owl Moon* pp. 10–14	methods of observation	Scientists acquire knowledge through observing.	observing ordinary places	oral language, writing, math
4. *I Wonder If I'll See a Whale* pp. 15–20	methods of observation	Scientists classify what they observe.	classifying birds	oral language, writing, math, art
5. *Tiger* pp. 21–25	methods of observation	Certain behaviors enable animals to meet needs.	observing animals	oral language, writing, poetry
6. *Alexander and the Wind-Up Mouse* pp. 26–30	diversity	Living things can be distinguished from nonliving things.	field trip obervations	oral language, writing, art, technology,
7. *The Very Hungry Caterpillar* pp. 31–36	patterns of change	Animals go through stages of development.	observing mealworms	oral language, writing, geography
8. *The Mixed-Up Chameleon* pp. 37–41	scale and structure change	Living things have properties that enable them to survive.	observing aquarium fish	oral language, writing, math, art

From *Science & Stories, Grades K–3*, published by GoodYearBooks. Copyright © 1994 Hilarie N. Staton and Tara McCarthy.

Literature	Major Theme	Science Concept	Investigations	Curricular Links
9. *Ox-Cart Man* pp. 42–46	systems and interactions	The sun is a source of heat energy.	heat and the seasons	oral language, writing, math
10. *The Legend of the Bluebonnet* pp. 47–51	systems and interactions	Water evaporates when heat is applied.	evaporating water; rainfall	oral language, writing, social studies, art
11. *Time of Wonder* pp. 52–57	systems and interactions	Wind is moving air.	wind direction	oral language, writing, math, music, art
12. *The Nightgown of the Sullen Moon* pp. 58–62	systems and interactions	The moon moves in an orbit around Earth. The earth and moon orbit the sun.	enactments of orbits	oral language, writing, social studies, math
13. *Katy and the Big Snow* pp. 63–67	energy and matter	Energy can be transferred by changing positions of objects.	moving different objects	oral language writing, art, geography, health
14. *The Magic Fan* pp. 68–73	energy and matter	Matter and energy interact to make change.	using air to move things	oral language, writing, math, art, social studies
15. *How to Dig a Hole to the Other Side of the World* pp. 74–78	energy and matter	Objects have distinctive properties.	classifying rocks	oral language, writing, social studies, geography
16. *Hill of Fire* pp. 79–83	patterns of change	Many materials change volume when heated.	making a mock volcano	oral language, writing, drama, social studies

Literature	Major Theme	Science Concept	Investigations	Curricular Links
17. *Gregory, the Terrible Eater* pp. 84–89	diversity	Living things thrive when their needs are met.	analyzing food charts	oral language, writing, social studies, math, art
18. *Bringing the Rain to Kapiti Plain* pp. 90–94	scale and structure	Plants have parts that function to help them thrive.	examining roots	oral language, writing, art, math, geography
19. *The Story of Jumping Mouse* pp. 95–99	systems and interactions	Our senses enable us to get information.	using senses to identify phenomena	oral language, writing, health, safety music
20. *Mandy* pp. 100–104	systems and interactions	Sound is made by vibrations that travel through matter.	making sounds in different ways	oral language, writing, social studies, poetry
21. *The Magic School Bus Inside the Human Body*, pp. 105–109	systems and interactions	Humans have properties that enable them to meet their own needs.	making a visual organizer	oral language, writing, social studies, poetry
22. *Letting Swift River Go* pp. 110–114	methods of observation	People solve problems through given processes.	solving immediate problems	oral language, writing, social studies, geography
23. *Heron Street* pp. 115–119	patterns of change	Change in one part of the environment causes changes in other parts.	a habitat field trip	oral language, writing, social studies
24. *Miss Rumphius* pp. 120–124	systems and interactions	Humans have the responsibility to use Earth's resources wisely.	planning an ecological project	oral language, writing, social studies, civics

From *Science & Stories*, Grades K-3, published by GoodYearBooks. Copyright © 1994 Hilarie N. Staton and Tara McCarthy.

HOW THE LESSONS IN THIS BOOK ARE ORGANIZED

Each lesson follows a teaching strategy that leads from enjoying literature to building science connections implicit in the literature. In turn, understandings in literature and science are applied to other areas of the curriculum.

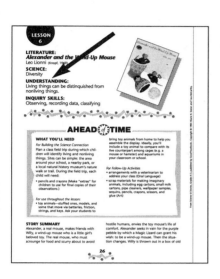

A statement of the Science Theme and Science Understanding in the lesson, and a list of the major inquiry skills the lesson helps develop.

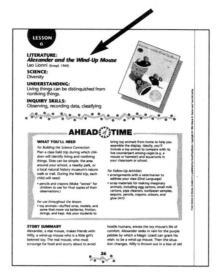

The book through which the science-literature connection will be made.

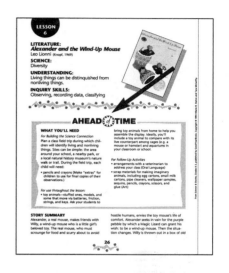

Special materials to get or preparations to make for specific parts of the lesson.

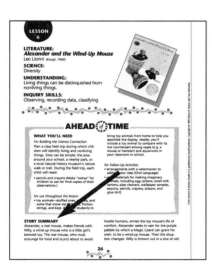

Story summary to indicate the general conceptual level of the literature.

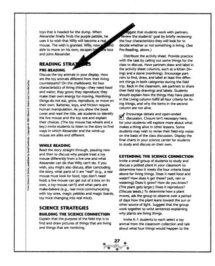

Suggestions to set the stage for the science and literature connections.

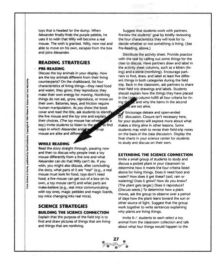

Suggestions to enhance comprehension and enjoyment of the literature.

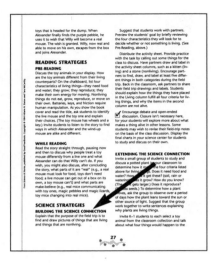

Instructions to carry out the science investigation.

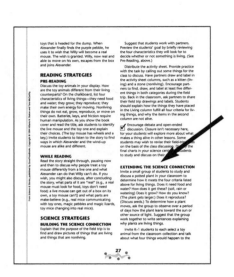

Suggestions for extending and enriching the basic science understanding for students with different abilities and interests.

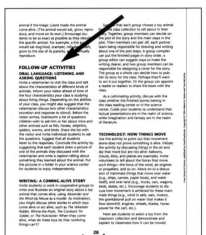

Activities for linking the science and literature understandings to other curricular areas.

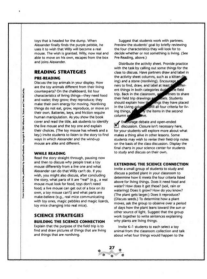

Ideas and strategies for assessment and elaboration.

Student reproducible for assessment or activity.

From *Science & Stories*, Grades K–3, published by GoodYearBooks. Copyright © 1994 Hilarie N. Staton and Tara McCarthy.

LITERATURE:
Witch Hazel
Alice Schertle (HarperCollins, 1991)

SCIENCE THEME:
Patterns of Change

UNDERSTANDING:
Plants go through stages of development.

INQUIRY SKILLS:
Observing, classifying

AHEAD *of* TIME

WHAT YOU'LL NEED

For Building the Science Connection
- many pumpkin seeds
- small, medium-sized, and large pumpkins

For Extending the Science Connection
- kernels from four to five ears of fresh, uncooked corn
- three or four ears of unshucked corn, of different sizes and with tassels intact

STORY SUMMARY
Johnny lives on a farm with his much-older brothers, Bill and Bart. When Johnny wants to help out with spring chores, the older boys amiably give him some pumpkin seeds to plant. Johnny plants the seeds and then makes a scarecrow to keep the birds away from the pumpkin vines. He dresses the scarecrow in a dress and a bonnet that he finds in musty trunk in the attic, and names her Witch Hazel. (Implicit but unstated in the story is that these were Johnny's now-deceased mother's clothes.) Though birds continue to eat the pumpkin blossoms, one pumpkin—protected by the folds of Witch Hazel's dress—continues to grow. At harvest time, Bill and Bart take their corn to the fair to sell, leaving Johnny alone. That night, in a dream, the boy visits Witch Hazel and sees her toss the pumpkin into the sky, where it hangs like a golden globe.

Then Hazel picks Johnny up, carries him home, and tucks him into bed. In the morning, there is only a broken pumpkin shell in the field, with its seeds scattered about. Johnny plants them. When his brothers return, they tell him that the biggest harvest moon ever had risen above the fairgrounds the night before. Johnny just smiles.

READING STRATEGIES
PRE-READING
As you show and discuss the book cover, make clear that this isn't a story about witches. Explain that witch hazel is a kind of wild flower that has a fresh, spicy aroma, and that Witch Hazel is also the name of the scarecrow in the picture. Point out the cornstalks in the foreground. Discuss what scarecrows are intended to protect. Ask students to listen to the story to find out what special things Witch Hazel protects.

WHILE READING

Pause now and then to discuss the progress from spring to fall of Johnny's pumpkin vines and the big brothers' corn crop. Invite students to tell about experiences they have had with growing plants outdoors. Stress the pattern: from seed to small plant to mature plant. Other patterns you might call attention to are the changing weather from spring to summer to fall and the repetition of what Bart and Bill say to Johnny: "You're too little. You're too young." At the conclusion of the story ask students what will happen to the pumpkin seeds in the ground, and how they know. You might also ask "Is Johnny growing up? What makes you think so?" (his changed attitude toward his brothers) "Is growing older a pattern too?"

SCIENCE STRATEGIES

BUILDING THE SCIENCE CONNECTION

On a table, arrange the pumpkins and pumpkin seeds in a left-to-right order that does not represent the real pattern of growth. For example, you might put the largest pumpkin first, then the small pumpkin, then the seeds, then the medium-sized pumpkin.

Invite pairs of volunteers to rearrange the sequence to show how Johnny's pumpkin began and grew. After the sequence is correctly displayed, put some of the pumpkin seeds right after the biggest pumpkin and elicit from students why this is part of the correct sequence. (The seeds come from inside the grown pumpkin and can be planted to get more pumpkins.) To firm up the concept, review the end of the story, where Johnny plants seeds that fell from the broken pumpkin. Invite students to label the final display with numbers to show sequence.

EXTENDING THE SCIENCE CONNECTION

Activity 1. Invite students to gather around and examine, touch, and sniff the unshucked ears of corn. Discuss likenesses, or patterns, that they find in all the ears—for example, the shape of the ears of corn, the rough feel of the husks, the feathery feel of the tassels, and the odor. Pull down the husk on one ear of corn so that students can see the pattern in which the kernels grow on the cob. Ask them to predict the pattern they'd see in the kernels on the other ears. Then shuck the corn to check if their predictions were accurate.

Invite students to handle the separate corn kernels and determine what part of the corn they came from by re-examining the whole ears. Then ask volunteers to find the things in the pumpkin display that are very much like the corn kernels (the pumpkin seeds). Continue by asking students to predict the pattern of growth of an ear of corn, starting with the kernel. Suggest that your readers review the pictures in *Witch Hazel* to see how corn grows over the course of the summer.

Activity 2. To create an ongoing display of the pattern most plants follow, invite students to bring from home the seeds of fresh fruits, such as apples, grapefruit, and peaches. In addition, children in suburban and rural areas can find tree seeds such as acorns, hazelnuts, and maple seeds. Make available junior nature encyclopedias, field guides, or seed and garden catalogues that have pictures of the mature plants (trees). Suggest that students work with partners to make montages that show the pattern of growth. On poster paper, have students tape or glue the seeds they've brought in, then draw pictures of the mature plants and the fruit or nuts they bear.

FOLLOW-UP ACTIVITIES

ORAL LANGUAGE: PATTERNS IN TIME

Discuss the patterns of the seasons in *Witch Hazel:* spring, summer, and fall. Ask students, "What will come next?" (winter). "How do you know?" (from experience). Then play a sequence game to reinforce the concept that time follows many natural patterns. Use any time patterns that you are teaching in your classroom. Prepare or obtain pictures that show

From *Science & Stories, Grades K-3*, published by GoodYearBooks. Copyright © 1994 Hilarie N. Staton and Tara McCarthy.

the steps of the sequence. Use a separate picture for each step. For example, draw and label pictures of the four seasons; make clock faces showing the hours in sequence; draw pictures of morning (sun rising and children rising), noon (the high noon sun and children playing outdoors), evening (the setting sun with children running home), and night (the dark sky, and children sleeping). With students who are reading on their own, use parts of calendar pages that have the names of the months and of the days of the week printed boldly.

Begin each version of the game by displaying the visuals in order and talking about them, using the names (summer, Tuesday, morning, or one o'clock). Ask children to say the names aloud with you in order several times. Then explain that you're going to "break the pattern," either by leaving something out or reversing the order. Ask students to listen for the place where the pattern breaks, and then correct you by telling the correct pattern. For example—(You): "Spring, summer, winter. What did I leave out of the pattern?" (Child) "You left out fall. The pattern is spring, summer, fall, winter." (You): "Monday, Tuesday, Thursday, Wednesday. What did I get in the wrong order?" (Child): "Thursday and Wednesday. It goes Monday, Tuesday, Wednesday, Thursday."

Since kids love to "trip up" the teacher, this game can go on for quite a while! Make sure your superstars don't monopolize the responses. After a few rounds with any time pattern, shy or hesitant students will be ready to get in on the action.

WRITING: PATTERNS IN SOUND
Invite students to work in cooperative learning groups of four or five to write nature poems that have end rhymes. Introduce the activity by reading such a poem. Accentuate the end rhymes and ask students to identify them. Here is an example by Christina Rossetti (emphasis is ours).

Fly away, fly away, over the *sea*,
Sun-loving swallow, for summer is *done*.
Come again, come again, come back to *me*,
Bringing the summer and bringing the *sun*.

Here is an example based on the book *Witch Hazel*:

Witch Hazel guards the pumpkin *seeds*.
These are things that Johnny *needs*.
Pumpkin vines will grow up *high*.
One pumpkin ends up in the *sky*.

Suggest that group members decide together on the subject of their nature poem. Then members can pair off to write rhyming lines on the subject. After group members share their lines, they can appoint two members to put the lines in an order that makes sense, while other members draw pictures to illustrate the poem. Before each group's spokesperson shares the poem with the class, ask the audience to listen for the words that make a sound pattern. You might record the presentations on tape for students to listen to and discuss later.

MATH/THINKING SKILLS: NUMBER PATTERNS
You can use the pumpkin seeds and corn kernels laid out on a table to set up predictable patterns that students can complete. Start with simple patterns like this one.

Ask students to lay out on the table "what comes next" (in the example above, one pumpkin seed), and then ask them how they knew what came next. Encourage students to use the word pattern in their explanations ("The pattern is one pumpkin seed and then one corn kernel and then one pumpkin seed.") Move on to more complex patterns, geared to your students' level of understanding. For example, this pattern is slightly more difficult than the one on the previous page.

This pattern requires a still higher level of recognition. Here the student has two factors to work with: the increasing number, plus the alternation of types of seeds that exhibit the number.

Invite interested students to use the seeds and kernels to make other patterns for their classmates to complete.

MUSIC: PATTERNS OF RHYTHM
As students listen to, sing along with, and tap out rhythm accompaniments to songs, ask them to listen to the rhythm patterns so that they can re-create these patterns with the rhythm instruments alone. Invite interested students to set up "What's That Song?" games, challenging classmates to guess the song title from the rhythm only.

ART: PATTERNS IN SHAPES
Distribute copies of Activity Sheet 1. Talk about the differences in the patterns of the three leaves shown at the top of the page: maple leaf, oak leaf, and birch leaf. Ask students to trace around the leaves at the top. Then, after they have cut out all the leaves on the sheet, ask

them to put the leaves in piles according to matching patterns. According to the abilities of your students, have them create two other pattern games to play with classmates.

Game 1. Students can make color trios, coloring three leaves red, three leaves brown, and three leaves green. The student mixes up the cards and then asks others to group leaves according to their colors.

Game 2. Partners can also group leaves according to size (small, medium, and big). Challenge interested students to find other possible patterns (such as leaves that have sharp edges and leaves that have smooth edges). Students can also paste the leaves on cardboard, then cut the cardboard leaves to make small jigsaw puzzles.

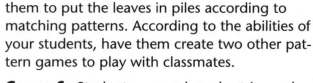

APPLYING THE SCIENCE CONCEPT:
Natural patterns pervade many of the stories used in this book. From time to time, ask students about the patterns they perceive as they read about them. For example, in *I Wonder If I'll See a Whale,* the main character learns to recognize individual whales by the unique patterns of their tails. In *Ox-Cart Man,* the family follows a year-round pattern of work. *The Magic School Bus Inside the Human Body* shows that there is a pattern to how our bodies work. *The Very Hungry Caterpillar* shows the pattern in the development of a butterfly. By identifying patterns, students codify concepts and themes in science. In addition, realizing that natural patterns exist and function predictably is emotionally reassuring to young children.

From *Science & Stories,* Grades K–3, published by GoodYearBooks. Copyright © 1994 Hilarie N. Staton and Tara McCarthy.

Witch Hazel

Name _____ Date _____

Directions
Trace the leaves and cut them out.

 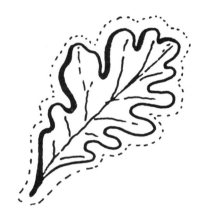 

Cut out these leaves too.

You can play games with your cutout leaves. Your teacher will tell you how.

LITERATURE:
Whistle for Willie
Ezra Jack Keats (Viking, 1964)

SCIENCE:
Methods of Observation

UNDERSTANDING:
Sounds move in all directions.

INQUIRY SKILLS:
Observing, classifying

AHEAD (of) TIME

WHAT YOU'LL NEED

For Building the Science Connection
- various sound-making objects such as a kitchen timer, a radio, a computer printer, or kitchen tongs
- various musical instruments, such as drums, autoharp, harmonica, triangle, guitar, tambourine, rattle, recorder, jingle bells
- various common objects to create sound, such as: tin cans, foil, plastic wrap, wooden blocks, books, plastic drinking glasses with and without water, pencils, ruler, spoons

For Follow-Up Activities
- audiotape recording of everyday sounds (Oral Language)
- tape recorder (Oral Language, Social Studies)

STORY SUMMARY

Peter wanted to whistle like the big kids. He especially wanted to whistle to his dog, Willie. Peter tried to whistle, but couldn't. He whirled around in circles, drew lines on walls, and tried to whistle again, but he still couldn't whistle. Peter went home and pretended to be his father, but he still could not whistle. He went back outside to find Willie and when he found him, Peter hid in a carton. Then Peter surprised both Willie and himself by whistling. Willie raced to him and they rushed home to share Peter's accomplishment with his parents. After that, Peter whistled all the way to the grocery store and back home again.

READING STRATEGIES

PRE-READING

Show students the cover of the book and read the title to them. Invite them to predict what the boy is trying to do. Have them predict who Willie is and who is going to be whistling. Have them suggest all the different ways people can whistle. Have volunteers display their talent. Then invite students to list all the reasons they can think of for whistling.

From *Science & Stories, Grades K–3,* published by GoodYearBooks. Copyright © 1994 Hilarie N. Staton and Tara McCarthy.

WHILE READING

Read the book to students. After a few pages, have the students predict what will happen next. At several places in the story, have students summarize what has happened so far. If students are unable to recall the events, use modeling to demonstrate the memory strategies you use, such as recalling pictures to help them remember. Recalling key actions is another good memory strategy.

SCIENCE STRATEGIES

BUILDING THE SCIENCE CONNECTION

Activity 1. Invite students to list all the sounds they have heard since they woke up this morning. Keep a class list. Discuss different ways to describe and categorize sounds, such as loud or soft sounds, nature or people sounds, and noisy or musical sounds. Use several sound-making objects, such as a kitchen timer, a radio, or kitchen tongs, to play sounds for students. Include some musical instruments and invite students to share any instruments they play. Encourage students to describe each sound in as many ways as possible. Play a guessing game by making a sound out of students' sight. Encourage students to describe it and guess what you are using to create the sound.

Activity 2. Have students work in small groups or with partners. Give each group two or three common objects. Invite groups to use these objects to make as many different sounds as possible. Encourage students to be creative about how they make sounds. If necessary, suggest students hit the object, use the object to strike another object, rub the objects together, or blow on an object. Invite the class to describe each sound as it is made. Have students use the same method to make a soft sound and a loud sound. Students can keep logs of how they create the sounds and share their findings with the class. Post these logs where other students can use them to repeat the sounds and create new ones.

EXTENDING THE SCIENCE CONNECTION

Activity 1. Related lessons in this book include those on senses for *Owl Moon* (page 10) and *The Story of Jumping Mouse* (page 95) as well as those on sound for *Mandy* (page 100). Invite students to read other books about sounds, such as Aliki's *Mary Bloom's,* Pamela Allen's *Bertie and the Bear,* Eric Carle's *The Very Busy Spider,* and Dayle-Ann Dobbs's *Wheel Away!*

Activity 2. Able or interested second- and third-graders can investigate how people make various sounds, such as whistling, humming, or speaking. They can write and illustrate an instruction sheet for making each type of sound.

FOLLOW-UP ACTIVITIES

ORAL LANGUAGE: ACTING SOUNDS

Play a guessing game with students, using an audiotape of everyday sounds. You might include a mixer, film projector, alarm clock, bus, and so on. The first time you play the tape give students clues to identify sources of the sounds. You might tell where the item is found or what it is used for. Replay the tape and stop after each sound. Have students create an action to represent that sound. They might whirl for a mixer or pantomime waking up for an alarm clock. Play the sounds on the tape in random order and have students do the action for that sound.

ORAL LANGUAGE: WHO'S ROARING NOW?

Have students form groups of four to five students. Assign each group an environment they have studied. Group members investigate the natural sounds in that environment and draw a mural showing the environment and some of the things that make sounds in it. For some environments, such as oceans or forests, environmental recordings are available. Invite group members to stand in front of the mural and re-create specific environmental sounds. Some

students may want to act out the sounds or have their classmates guess what is creating the sound.

WRITING: SOUND JOURNAL

Encourage students to stop and listen four times a day and make note of each sound they hear. They can record their findings using words or pictures. Invite students to share their findings in small groups. Each group can create a master list or picture chart of the sounds they've heard. Using this list, group members can write short reports about daily sounds. Invite each group to share its findings with the class.

WRITING: I HEAR A RIDDLE

Review all the sound words students have encountered while studying sound. Create a class list, if you don't already have one. Discuss onomatopoeia (words that are spelled to imitate a sound) and other sound words. Read to students Mary O'Neill's book *What Is That Sound?* and share comic book sound effects such as *pow, crash,* and *bam.* With the class, write several riddles that use sound words or onomatopoeia. An example might be:

> *Thump* goes my tail when I'm happy.
> *Woof!* goes my voice when I'm angry.
> *Howl,* I say when the moon's full. (a dog)

Have pairs of students write their own sound riddles with their own sound words. They can try their riddles on other pairs of students. You can also use these riddles as part of the class's daily writing or reading assignments.

SOCIAL STUDIES: A COMMUNITY WALK

Take students on a walk through the community. Carry a tape recorder and record the sounds you hear. Where possible, stop, listen, and discuss these sounds. Acquaint students with warning sounds, such as sirens, and what each means. When you return to the classroom, play the tape and have students identify the sounds. Invite small groups of students to create a story that uses the sounds from the tape as well as dialog that they invent. Allow groups to present these skits or read their stories to the class.

APPLYING THE SCIENCE CONCEPT:

Hand out Activity Sheet 2. Explain each of the pictured sounds, but do not discuss or describe the sounds. Define the categories LOUD and SOFT. Use your voice to demonstrate the difference. Point out that you can hear a loud sound far away, because more energy has gone into making it. You must be close and quiet to hear a soft sound. Have students cut out the sounds and paste them under the category that best describes them. Then have students draw two more sounds for each category. Encourage students to share their choices and tell why they made them.

From *Science & Stories*, Grades K-3, published by GoodYearBooks. Copyright © 1994 Hilarie N. Staton and Tara McCarthy.

Whistle for Willie

Name _____ Date _____

WHAT DO I HEAR?

Directions
Cut out the pictures. Decide if each makes a LOUD or soft sound. Paste it under the correct head-ing. Then draw two more things that make LOUD sounds and two more that make soft sounds.

LOUD SOUNDS	soft sounds

LITERATURE:
Owl Moon
Jane Yolen (Philomel, 1987)

SCIENCE:
Methods of Observation

UNDERSTANDING:
Scientists acquire knowledge through observing.

INQUIRY SKILLS:
Observing, classifying

AHEAD *of* TIME

WHAT YOU'LL NEED

For Building the Science Connection
- extra paper for making observation sheets
- (optional) flip chart and marker for summarizing observations

For Follow-Up Activities
- arrangements with teachers and other school personnel for student observation posts (Oral Language)

STORY SUMMARY
Late one winter night, a young child goes with her father to look for owls. They walk toward the still, snow-covered woods after hearing trains and dogs sing through the cold air. They walk silently, leaving footprints in the snow and trailing shadows. Pa stops, searches the sky, and imitates the cry of the great horned owl. Nothing answers, so the pair continues into the woods. As they go deeper into the woods, the child must ignore the cold and deep shadows and stay quiet, all hoping to see an owl. Then, in a moonlit clearing, Pa calls again. They listen and look carefully. Soon they hear a call echoing though the trees. Pa calls again. The owl comes closer until it separates from the tree shadows and flies over the silent father and child. The light from Pa's flashlight catches it landing. The owl and humans stare at each other. Then, silently, the owl flies away, and the people return home.

READING STRATEGIES
PRE-READING
Show students the cover of the book. Ask them to imagine what they might hear or see in snowy woods on a winter's night. Encourage them to list anything they can think of regardless of whether their answers are correct. Then have them predict what they think the book is about, since it is called *Owl Moon*. Encourage them to use the cover and title for clues. Finally, have them try to think of everything they know about owls. Introduce the word *owling* and ask what they think it might mean (going out at night to observe owls).

WHILE READING

Read the book to students. For the first reading, allow students to enjoy the story and language. Encourage them to share what they liked about the book. Before you reread the book, ask students to think about these questions: What did the people see and hear? How did they act in order to find the owl? How did the child feel at different times in their walk?

Reread the book and discuss the answers to these questions with the students. For some students you may need to stop while you are reading the story to answer the questions with them.

SCIENCE STRATEGIES

BUILDING THE SCIENCE CONNECTION

With the class, create a list of all the things the father and child saw in the woods that night. Then invite students to add things from the pictures that the writer does not mention. Discuss observation methods, such as sitting quietly, listening carefully, looking all around, and making notes on what you see. Ask the children to be silent for one minute while observing everything possible. When the time is up, invite them to share all the sights and sounds they observed.

Have students create blank observation sheets like the following.

OBSERVATION SHEET

Place:

Time:

What I saw:

What I heard:

Ask each student to make three copies. Have each student make three observations, in different places outside the classroom, at different times of the day. The observations can take place in the lunchroom, at recess, at a family meal, or early in the morning. Encourage students to make notes, using either words or pictures, on their observation sheets. Suggest they be as quiet as possible for as long as possible so they can observe all the sights and sounds. After all the observations are done, invite students to share them with the class. Meanwhile, keep track on a large class chart the sights, sounds, tastes, touches, and smells that fill the students' world. Invite students to discuss unusual observations as well as those that were expected.

EXTENDING THE SCIENCE CONNECTION

Activity 1. This observation activity can be done in conjunction with other observation activities, such as those suggested in the lesson on *Whistle for Willie* (page 6) or *I Wonder If I'll See a Whale* (page 15), or in conjunction with lessons on the senses, such as those suggested in the lesson on *The Story of Jumping Mouse* (page 95) or *Mandy* (page 100). Second- and third-grade students can conduct more detailed observations. These might include observing a process (such as water boiling) or the same place over a period of time. Both younger and older students can research and observe (if location and time of year allow) a natural setting both before and after dark. They can compare and contrast what they learn about nightlife with what they know about life during the day. They can make two murals which include the same animals and what they do at the different times.

Activity 2. All students can do additional activities about seasons and winter using books such as *Ox-Cart Man* (page 42) or *Katy and the Big Snow* (page 63).

Activity 3. Third-grade students might enjoy researching owls. Books such as Farley Mowat's *Owls in the Family* describe the habits of these beautiful, but seldom seen birds. Investigating the contents of an owl pellet (available through science supply catalogs) can give students insight into the habits of these animals.

FOLLOW-UP ACTIVITIES

ORAL LANGUAGE: WHAT DID YOU SEE?

Make arrangements with another teacher, the cafeteria, the school office, or some other place in the school for students to observe. Over several days, allow one student at a time to spend five minutes silently observing the location. Students should make notes (words or pictures) so that they remember what they see and hear. Have the class make a list of everything seen or heard. Encourage students to draw the conclusion that different people notice different things. Reread *Owl Moon.* Emphasize the fact that the father and child were looking for something specific.

Have students form small groups and assign each group another place around the school to observe. Have each group member choose one section of that place to observe. For instance, one group might observe the front of the room, while another observes the back. Each group compiles a list of everything its members observed. Students can also use this list to make a picture of the place they observed. Have each group present its final observation list and picture to the class. Encourage the class to draw the conclusion that it is much easier to observe within a limited range than to try to observe everything that is going on.

WRITING: WALK WITH ME. WHAT DO YOU SEE?

Create cooperative learning groups of four or five students. Take each group on a walk. This can be a nature walk, a walk through certain parts of the school, or around the neighborhood. All groups can go on the same walk, or each group can take a different route. When each group returns, have students make lists of what they saw along the way. After their list is complete, each member should write a short paragraph describing something on the list. After their paragraphs are completed, members share them with their group. Encourage the stu-

dents to suggest more colorful, detailed descriptions. Each member revises his or her writing and makes a clean copy with an illustration. Collect each group's illustrations into a Walk Book. These books can be shared with the class and kept in a reading corner for everyone to enjoy.

MATH: WORD PROBLEMS

Use modeling to show the class how to write a simple math word problem about something that they observed. You might say:

When I was in the library yesterday, I saw two children bring back books. This would make a good math problem. I could ask about how many books they brought back. Let's see. Two children came to the library. One brought back two books and the other brought back four books. What can I ask? I know! How many books did the librarian have to check in? That's an easy problem!

After you have modeled this process, invite volunteers to suggest an entirely different situation, with different details and questions. Do several problems with the class. Then have students form small groups and invite each group to submit four word problems. Create a homework or classwork sheet using these problems.

APPLYING THE SCIENCE CONCEPT

✓ Hand out Activity Sheet 3. Explain that students should write down (in words or pictures) everything they would see, hear, smell, taste, or touch if they were the child in the picture. Give students a time limit. This can be a cooperative activity.

From *Science & Stories*, Grades K–3, published by GoodYearBooks. Copyright © 1994 Hilarie N. Staton and Tara McCarthy.

Owl Moon

Name _____ Date _____

USING YOUR SENSES

Directions

Write down everything you would see, hear, taste, smell, or touch if you were the child in the picture on the next page.

What I See	What I Hear	What I Smell	What I Taste	What I Touch

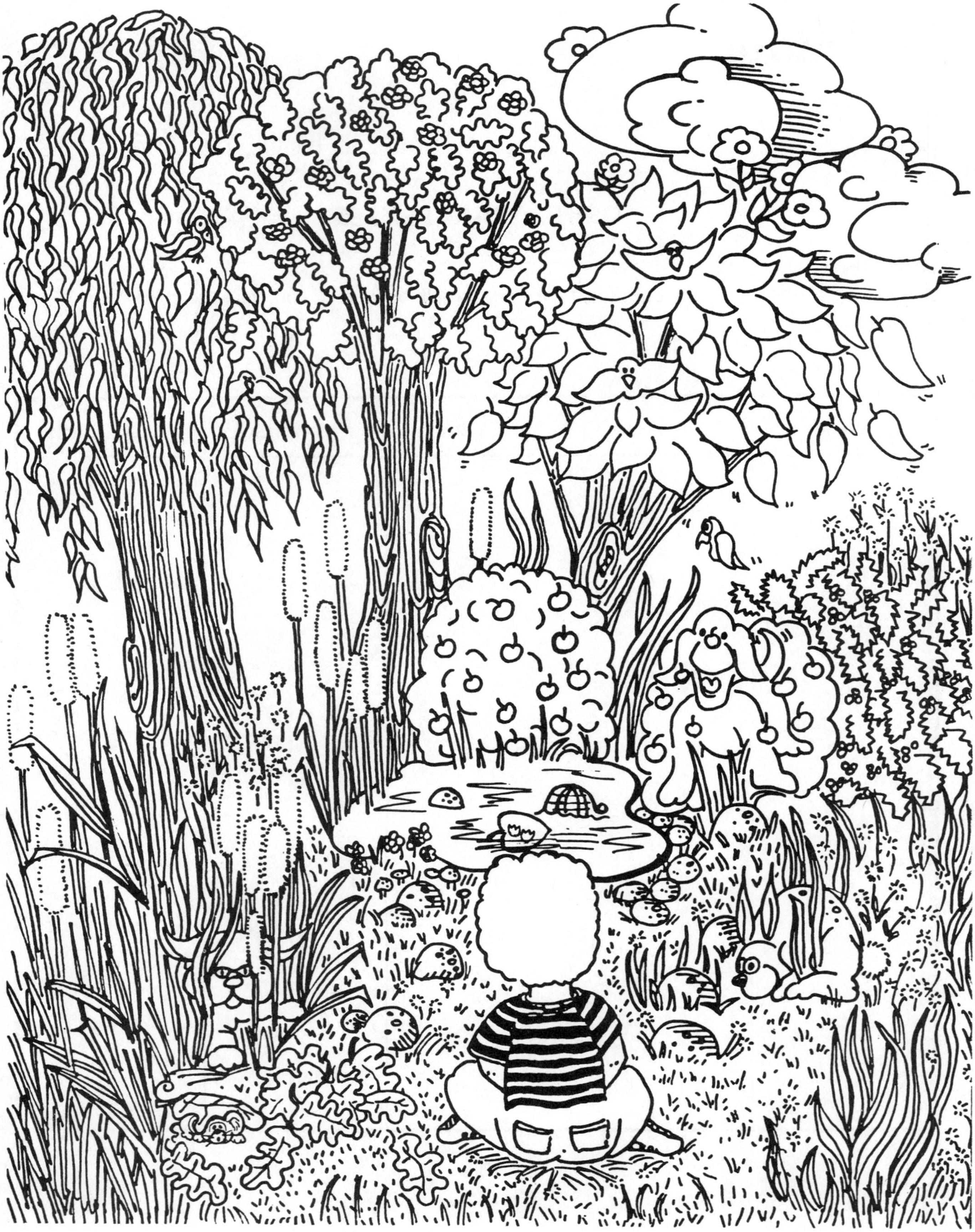

From *Science & Stories*, Grades K-3, published by GoodYearBooks. Copyright © 1994 Hilarie N. Staton and Tara McCarthy.

LESSON 4

LITERATURE:
I Wonder If I'll See a Whale
Frances Ward Weller (Philomel, 1991)

SCIENCE:
Methods of Observation

UNDERSTANDING:
Scientists classify what they observe.

INQUIRY SKILLS:
Observing, recording data, interpreting data, classifying

AHEAD *of* TIME

WHAT YOU'LL NEED

For Building the Science Connection
- a field trip or nature walk or
- a bird feeder and feed to attract a variety of birds

For Follow-Up Activities
- magazine or coloring book pictures showing detailed nature scenes (Oral Language)
- animal pictures (Oral Language)
- materials for collages, including paper, pencils, crayons, scraps of cloth, leaves, twigs, glue (Art)

STORY SUMMARY

A young girl goes out on a boat hoping to see a whale, since humpback whales migrate through the area. They pass by so often that the boat's crew can identify each whale by the markings on its tail. The girl watches dolphins play, but wonders if she'll ever see a whale. When spouts are sighted, the boat travels toward them. A mother and baby whale appear and disappear. Clouds of bubbles from their blowhole appear as some whales herd small fish. Suddenly, the humpbacks surface to feed on these fish. Then all the whales submerge, except Trunk. He reappears and breaches several times. He waves his tail and comes up to observe his visitors. A reverent moment occurs as the sea mammal and the child stare at each other. When the boat finally leaves, the girl promises to return to visit her new friend.

READING STRATEGIES

PRE-READING

Invite students to share everything they know about whales. Keep a list of these facts. Then invite students to list questions they would like answered about whales. Keep these questions visible so students can refer to them during the reading and later activities. After students have discussed whales, ask them to suggest ways people, especially scientists, learn about whales.

WHILE READING

After reading a page or two of the story, invite

students to predict what will happen next. Discuss the clues that lead them to make each prediction. As soon as you finish reading the story, encourage students to summarize it. If necessary, explain that a summary of the story does not need to include the factual information about whales. Give students examples of how the action on several pages can be summarized in a few words.

SCIENCE STRATEGIES
BUILDING THE SCIENCE CONNECTION

Reread the book. Stop after each page and ask students to identify the facts about whales. Add these to the list of facts the students already know. For older students, organize the list into specific categories, such as feeding habits, body forms, and sounds. After the list is complete, ask students how the crew of the boat and scientists learn about the whales. Help students draw the conclusion that careful observations are necessary to learn about animals. To remember their observations, scientists need to keep careful, detailed notes about what they see.

Explain to students that they are going to become scientists who are studying animals. The rest of this activity will use birds as the animals, but you can use other types of animals if you take a field trip to a zoo, farm, or pet shop. Before observing the birds, discuss their general characteristics and encourage students to make a list of possible bird characteristics. Create a class chart with the general characteristics they would like to observe (beak shape, feathers, feet). Be sure students are realistic. For instance, they probably won't be able to observe nest types, but they will be able to observe body size and color. Invite students to suggest words that could be used for each category. Make a small version of the class chart, so students can take notes directly on the chart.

Suggest that students work with partners, so one member can observe while the other takes notes. Then the two can switch roles. Do some

trial observations with the whole class observing bird pictures. After students take notes on the pictures, encourage them to share the facts they wrote down and the descriptive words they used. You may want to discuss how students can use abbreviations to write details quickly.

After they've practiced observing pictures, have students observe live birds. Take a field trip to a zoo, wildlife area, or park. Other options include visiting a local resident who has a very active bird feeder that is easily observed or building a bird feeder and placing it outside the classroom windows. Be sure to use a feed that will attract a variety of birds. Students can observe and take notes about the birds at the feeder at various times over several days. Encourage them to look for facts about each characteristic on their chart for the birds they observe.

After the observations are complete, have the partners review their information and share it with the class. Place the information on the class chart. Invite students to suggest different ways birds can be classified or grouped. Have each group classify the birds by one criterion, such as size, and then group them further by choosing another characteristic, such as beak size. In order to see the relationship between these groups, a chart like the one on the next page can be constructed.

Have partners write descriptions of the birds using only their categories. Read the descriptors to the class as part of a guessing game. Volunteers can try to identify the bird in as few clues (categories) as possible.

EXTENDING THE SCIENCE CONNECTION
Activity 1. Second- and third-grade students can use the information about humpback whales to begin research about other whales, ocean animals, or the ocean environment.

Activity 2. Interested or more able third-grade students can do more complex classification activities. They can develop the criteria for

From *Science & Stories*, Grades K-3, published by GoodYearBooks. Copyright © 1994 Hilarie N. Staton and Tara McCarthy.

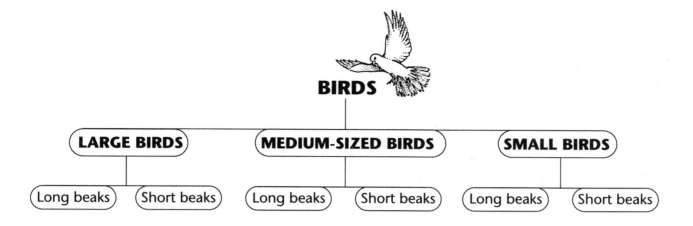

BIRDS

LARGE BIRDS
- Long beaks
- Short beaks

MEDIUM-SIZED BIRDS
- Long beaks
- Short beaks

SMALL BIRDS
- Long beaks
- Short beaks

From *Science & Stories*, Grades K–3, published by GoodYearBooks. Copyright © 1994 Hilarie N. Staton and Tara McCarthy.

a classification system for a specific list of animals. You might suggest they begin by separating the animals into two categories, such as vertebrates and invertebrates or warm-blooded and cold-blooded animals. After students research and categorize the animals, they can make further divisions using other characteristics. Students can also make charts of their classification systems to share with the class. Their presentations should include the criteria they used to develop each level in their systems.

FOLLOW-UP ACTIVITIES

ORAL LANGUAGE: QUICK! WHAT DID YOU SEE?

Collect a series of pictures that shows scenes familiar to students. These might be large photographs or large, simple illustrations from books or magazines. Show one picture to the class for a limited amount of time (the amount of time will depend on the age and visual memory skills of your students). Then hide the picture and ask students to recall what they saw. Create a class list and then check it against the picture. As they view the picture again, allow students to add missing details to the class list. Once the students feel comfortable with this game, have them break into pairs and play it with each other. Players can keep track of the number of items they recall to see if they remember more than on their first attempt. Encourage students to express what they see in complete sentences.

ORAL LANGUAGE: FINDING CATEGORIES, TEACHING RULES

Divide students into groups of three to five. Give each group a stack of animal pictures which includes some fish, some mammals, and some insects. Tell students that they must divide these pictures into three categories: fish, mammals, and insects. After they've separated the pictures into categories, have students examine each set and write three rules to go into each category. For example, "Always has six legs" would apply to insects. When they're done, give students another set of pictures, which they must fit into the categories they have created, using the rules they've written. Students must edit and add to the rules so that every picture fits one of the three categories. Each group creates some type of visual to show their classification system. Have each group share their classification system and rules with the class.

WRITING: KEEPING A SCIENTIFIC JOURNAL

Have each student keep an observation journal for at least a week. Students can record their observations about one specific animal or about all the animals they see each day. Invite students to share their journal entries with a "fellow scientist." Suggest that partners keep a list of the best descriptive phrases they have used and share them with at least one other team. In their final entry, encourage students o summarize what they learned about animals and about the process of observing.

MATH: GRAPHING WHAT WE'VE SEEN

As a class, in small groups, or with partners, have students create pictographs or bar graphs to show how many animals they see each day for a week. They can graph one type of animal, such as dogs, or compare two different types, such as dogs and cats. Each group should write questions to go with its graph. After their graphs and questions are complete, invite students to share them with the class. Include them as activities in an independent math center.

ART: CREATING A SCENE

Invite students to create collage scenes using a variety of objects, such as found objects (pencils, paper, twigs, etc.), magazine illustrations, or their own drawings or paintings. After students share their scenes with the class, the scenes can be used to play games such as "Quick! What do you see?" Students might also write journal entries about other students' scenes.

APPLYING THE SCIENCE CONCEPT:

☑ Hand out Activity Sheet 4. Suggest students examine the scene as if they were scientists. They are to write a scientific journal entry, giving their observations and categorizing some of the things they see. Invite students to color the picture before they begin the activity, so that colors can be used as categories, if desired.

From *Science & Stories*, Grades K-3, published by GoodYearBooks. Copyright © 1994 Hilarie N. Staton and Tara McCarthy.

I Wonder If I'll See a Whale

Name _____ Date _____

DEEP IN THE WOODS

Directions

You are a scientist studying the forest shown on the next page. Write a journal entry about what you see. Create at least two categories for the things you see and list three things in each category.

Journal Entry:

What I Observed:

Category 1	Category 2
_____	_____
_____	_____
_____	_____

From *Science & Stories*, Grades K-3, published by GoodYearBooks. Copyright © 1994 Hilarie N. Staton and Tara McCarthy.

LESSON 5

LITERATURE:
Tiger
Judy Allen (Candlewick Press, 1992)

SCIENCE:
Methods of Observation

UNDERSTANDING:
Certain behaviors enable animals to meet their needs.

INQUIRY SKILLS:
Observing, recording data, interpreting data, generalizing

AHEAD *of* TIME

WHAT YOU'LL NEED

For Building the Science Connection
• drawing and writing materials

For Follow-Up Activities
• a videotape about animal behavior

STORY SUMMARY

In a small village in Asia, rumor has it that a tiger prowls in the oak woods beyond the rice fields. In spite of the fact that it's against the law, the villagers wish to kill the tiger: folklore says that eating tiger meat will make you brave; and a tiger skin can be sold for a great deal of money. Only one child, Lee, wants the tiger to go on living. He dislikes the hunter the villagers hire to hunt down and shoot the tiger for them. The hunter himself changes his mind as he tracks and observes the tiger. It kills only to eat, and the hunter is moved by the animal's grace and skill as it seeks to survive in the woods. In the long run, the only "shot" the hunter takes at the tiger is with a camera. Returning to the village, the hunter says he saw no tiger. With a wink, he lets Lee know the truth.

READING STRATEGIES

PRE-READING

After showing and reading the book cover to students, invite them to contribute ideas to a poster paper list titled "What We Think Tigers Are Like." Ask students where they got their information. After recording students' ideas, ask them to listen to the story to find out whether or not their ideas are correct. For discussion after students have heard the story, prepare two more charts headed "What the Story Tells Us About Tigers" and "Other Things We'd Like to Find Out About Tigers."

WHILE READING

Read the story straight through, pausing when necessary to explain difficult words, such as

21

prey, rumor, profit, hindquarters, and *undulated.* Encourage students to suggest definitions from the context of the words.

At a couple of points in the story, pause to ask students why the hunter doesn't shoot the tiger when he gets chances to do so. Help students understand that the hunter is learning things about tigers by observing one in action, and that he's beginning to like and admire the tiger and realize that it presents no danger to humans.

Ask "How does the hunter use his knowledge to help keep the tiger safe?" The conclusion of the story presents an opportunity to discuss values, if you so wish. The hunter deliberately misleads the villagers into thinking that no tiger exists in the oak woods. You might discuss why the hunter wanted to mislead the villagers, whether it was right to do so, and what students would have done and said had they been the hunter. Discuss Lee's feelings and insights. How does he feel when he knows the tiger is still alive? Why does he feel this way? How have his attitudes about the hunter changed?

After reading the story, go over the students' "What We Think Tigers Are Like" list and ask them to cross out any ideas that the story has indicated to be incorrect, and (*) any ideas that the story substantiates. Then ask them to fill in the second chart "What the Story Tells Us About Tigers" with new facts they learned from the story. Encourage students to fill in the chart "Things We'd Like to Find Out About Tigers" with their remaining questions. Keep this chart for students to use when they do the Follow-Up writing activity.

SCIENCE STRATEGIES
BUILDING THE SCIENCE CONNECTION
Explain the purpose of the activity: to observe an animal and to record with words and pictures how the animal acts in its habitat, or environment. Initiate the activity by brainstorming a chalkboard list of animals that

people might observe in your area. For example, city children can observe birds, squirrels, insects, and pets. Suburban children can observe the former, plus deer, rabbits, toads, frogs, garter snakes, and chipmunks. Children who live in rural areas have a vast assortment of animals to choose from for observation. You might enlist parents or other family members at home to help with the assignment. Stress that observation means "watching from a safe distance." (Remind students that the hunter in *Tiger* did not get very close to the tiger! The not-too-close caution both protects the observer and helps to ensure that the animal will behave in a more natural manner.)

Distribute Activity Sheet 5 and go over the directions and labels. Allow three or four independent observation periods outside of your regular school schedule for students to complete the activity. You might make extra copies of the sheet for students who wish to re-record their field observations in an edited and "cleaned-up" form.

✔ As students share their completed activities with classmates, ask them to focus on this main idea: "What I have learned about the animal that I didn't know before." Encourage the classroom audience to ask questions of the observer, such as "How long did you watch?" "How far away were you from the animal?" "Do you think the animal saw you? If it did, what happened then?" Also encourage listeners to tell what they have learned from their classmates' observations. Conclude the activity by discussing how students have performed as scientists do: they have observed and made records to find out more about living things. Loop back to the book *Tiger* by discussing where the hunter observed the tiger (in its natural environment) and how he made a record by taking photographs.

From *Science & Stories, Grades K–3,* published by GoodYearBooks. Copyright © 1994 Hilarie N. Staton and Tara McCarthy.

EXTENDING THE SCIENCE CONNECTION

Show a videotape about animal behavior. Preface the viewing by discussing the topic, asking students what they hope to learn from the film, and listing their questions on the chalkboard. After the viewing, students can check the list to see what questions were answered. Also discuss any techniques that showed how the filmmakers were observing and recording as scientists do. Discuss how the narrator or filmmaker seemed to feel about the animal being observed.

FOLLOW-UP ACTIVITIES

ORAL LANGUAGE: THE CONTRADICTION GAME

This activity for seven or eight players gives students an opportunity to state what they know about animals they and their classmates have been studying. The game appeals to children because they love to "contradict," and in this context can do so with some knowledge. Prepare for the game by writing on slips of paper obviously false statements about animals your students have become familiar with through the book *Tiger* and the foregoing activities. Examples based on *Tiger* include "The tiger's favorite food is people," "Tigers like to live in villages," and "Tigers are afraid of water." Your other false statements will depend on what animals your students have listed on their Activity Sheets. Examples include "Deer are very friendly and like to come up close to people," "All big dogs chase people," "Cats are always awake," and "Snakes crawl up to people and bite them."

Put the statement slips in a box or bag in the center of the playing circle. Each player in turn chooses a slip and reads the statement, perhaps with your help. The player then contradicts the statement ("No, it isn't!" or "No, they don't!") and then makes a true statement about the situation. ("A tiger's favorite food is other wild animals," "Tigers like to live alone in the woods.") This isn't a win-or-lose game; encourage players to help one another frame the correct response before moving on to the next play.

WRITING: A WILD CAT BOOK

Invite students to work in groups to write and illustrate a factual book about tigers or other wild cats. Introduce the activity by reviewing with students their "Things We'd Like To Find Out About Tigers" chart (see While Reading). On the chalkboard, list other wild cats, such as puma, cheetah, leopard, jaguar, and lion. Ask each group to choose one of the wild cats to study and tell about in their book.

Group members can work together to revise the "Things We'd Like to Find Out About. . ." list to add queries about the wild cats they've chosen. Then each group member can choose one of the questions to research and answer via nonfiction books and general and nature encyclopedias. Answers can be in the form of paragraphs or sentences. The group can appoint two members as editors to help others revise and edit their writing. This done, each group member can make an illustration to accompany the text. Groups can appoint members to sequence the pages, make and illustrate a cover, and write a Table of Contents.

After groups share their wild cat books with the class, discuss how the wild cats are alike and different. Talk about any hazards they face as they cope with changes in their surroundings. Also discuss the sources students used as they created their books, including factual accounts by people who have observed and made records of these animals in their natural surroundings.

Students will also enjoy comparing the behavior of wild cats with their own pet cats. Help students to see that wild cats depend on wild food in their environment, while domestic cats can usually count on being fed by their owners. Put the completed books on a table in your reading center or science center for student partners to read and discuss on their own.

LITERATURE: POEMS ABOUT CATS

There are plenty of them! Introduce the activity by reading William Blake's *"The Tiger."* While your students might not understand all the references or words in this poem, they will be interested in the first lines ("Tiger, tiger, burning bright/In the forests of the night") and sense that it's not a scientific report, but rather one poet's impression of a tiger. Discuss how poets tell about things in different ways than scientists do: poets aim to build word pictures and create feelings with their words, while scientists concentrate on the facts.

Put several poetry anthologies on a table in your reading center. Invite poetry partners to find cat poems they like and to practice saying them aloud. Some students might want to learn poems by heart to present to the class. Encourage students to write their own poems about different kinds of cats, based on what they have learned about them so far. Challenge interested students to write a poem about the cat star of the book *Tiger*. After students read their poems to classmates, put the poems in a folder in your reading center for students to read and discuss independently.

APPLYING THE SCIENCE CONCEPT:

Suggest that students watch nature programs on TV and report to class-mates three or four facts they learned about animals or plants. Challenge interested students to note how the filmmaker collected information and to give their opinions as to whether he or she gathered the facts through direct observation.

From *Science & Stories*, Grades K-3, published by GoodYearBooks. Copyright © 1994 Hilarie N. Staton and Tara McCarthy.

Tiger

Name _____ Date _____

OBSERVING AN ANIMAL

Directions
Write the name of the aminal. Watch the animal. Then draw a picture to go with each sentence.

The animal I am observing is a _____.

1. This shows the animal getting its food.

2. This shows where the animal has a home, or shelter.

3. This shows the animal when it is moving.

4. This shows the animal when it is resting.

5. This shows something the animal is not afraid of.

6. This shows something the animal is afraid of.

LITERATURE:
Alexander and the Wind-Up Mouse
Leo Lionni (Knopf, 1969)

SCIENCE:
Diversity

UNDERSTANDING:
Living things can be distinquished from nonliving things.

INQUIRY SKILLS:
Observing, recording data, classifying

From *Science & Stories*, Grades K-3, published by GoodYearBooks. Copyright © 1994 Hilarie N. Staton and Tara McCarthy.

AHEAD of TIME

WHAT YOU'LL NEED

For Building the Science Connection

Plan a class field trip during which children will identify living and nonliving things. Sites can be simple: the area around your school, a nearby park, or a local natural history museum's nature walk or trail. During the field trip, each child will need:

• pencils and crayons (Make "extras" for children to use for final copies of their observations.)

For use throughout the lesson:

• toy animals—stuffed ones, models, and some that move via batteries, friction, strings, and keys. Ask your students to bring toy animals from home to help you assemble the display. Ideally, you'll include a toy animal to compare with its live counterpart among cages (e.g. a mouse or hamster) and aquariums in your classroom or school.

For Follow-Up Activities

• arrangements with a veterinarian to address your class (Oral Language)
• scrap materials for making imaginary animals, including egg cartons, small milk cartons, pipe cleaners, wallpaper samples, sequins, pencils, crayons, scissors, and glue (Art)

STORY SUMMARY

Alexander, a real mouse, makes friends with Willy, a wind-up mouse who is a little girl's beloved toy. The real mouse, who must scrounge for food and scurry about to avoid hostile humans, envies the toy mouse's life of comfort. Alexander seeks in vain for the purple pebble by which a Magic Lizard can grant his wish: to be a wind-up mouse. Then the situation changes. Willy is thrown out in a box of old

toys that is headed for the dump. When Alexander finally finds the purple pebble, he uses it to wish that Willy will become a real mouse. The wish is granted. Willy, now real and able to move on his own, escapes from the box and joins Alexander.

READING STRATEGIES

PRE-READING
Discuss the toy animals in your display. How are the toy animals different from their living counterparts? On the chalkboard, list four characteristics of living things—they need food and water; they grow; they reproduce; they make their own energy for moving. Nonliving things do not eat, grow, reproduce, or move on their own. Batteries, keys, and friction require human manipulation. As you show the book cover and read the title, ask students to identify the live mouse and the toy one and explain their choices. (The toy mouse has wheels and a key.) Invite students to listen to the story to find ways in which Alexander and the wind-up mouse are alike and different.

WHILE READING
Read the story straight through, pausing now and then to discuss why people treat a toy mouse differently from a live one and what Alexander can do that Willy can't do. If you wish, you might also discuss, after concluding the story, what parts of it are "real" (e.g., a real mouse must look for food, toys don't need food; a live mouse can get out of a box on its own, a toy mouse can't) and what parts are make-believe (e.g., real mice communicating with toy ones, magic pebbles and magic lizards, toy mice changing into real mice).

SCIENCE STRATEGIES

BUILDING THE SCIENCE CONNECTION
Explain that the purpose of the field trip is to find and draw pictures of things that are living and things that are nonliving.

Suggest that students work with partners. Preview the students' goal by briefly reviewing the four characteristics they will look for to decide whether or not something is living. (See Pre-Reading, above.)

Distribute the activity sheet. Provide practice with the task by calling out some things for the class to discuss. Have partners draw and label in the activity sheet columns, such as a kitten (living) and a stone (nonliving). Encourage partners to find, draw, and label at least five different things in both categories during the field trip. Back in the classroom, ask partners to share their field trip drawings and labels. Students should explain how the things they have placed in the Living column fulfill all four criteria for living things, and why the items in the second column are not alive.

✓ Encourage debate and open-ended discussion. Closure isn't necessary here, for your students will explore more about what makes a thing alive in other lessons. Some students may wish to revise their field-trip notes on the basis of the class discussion. Display the final charts in your science center for students to study and discuss on their own.

EXTENDING THE SCIENCE CONNECTION
Invite a small group of students to study and discuss a potted plant in your classroom to determine how it meets the four criteria listed above for living things. Does it need food and water? How does it get these? (soil, rain or watering) Does it grow? How do you know? (The plant gets larger.) Does it reproduce? (Discuss seeds.) To determine how a plant moves, ask the group to observe over a period of days how the plant leans toward the sun or other source of light. Suggest that the group work together to write sentences explaining why plants are living things.

Invite K–1 students to each select a toy animal from the classroom collection and talk about what four things would happen to the animal if the Magic Lizard made the animal come alive. (The animal would eat, grow, reproduce, and move on its own.) Encourage students to be as exact as possible as they describe the specific animal. For example, a live puppy would eat dog food, scamper, roll, sleep, bark, grow to the size of its parents, and eventually reproduce.

FOLLOW-UP ACTIVITIES

ORAL LANGUAGE: LISTENING AND ASKING QUESTIONS

Invite a veterinarian to visit the class and talk about the characteristics of different kinds of animals. Inform your visitor ahead of time of the four characteristics your class is studying about living things. Depending on the abilities of your class, you might also suggest that the veterinarian discuss two other characteristics: excretion and response to stimuli. Before the visitor arrives, brainstorm a list of questions children wish to ask him or her about mice and other animals such as fish, horses, dolphins, spiders, worms, and birds. Share the list with the visitor and invite individual students to ask the questions. Suggest that all students listen to the responses. Conclude the activity by suggesting that each student draw a picture of one of the animals they discussed with the veterinarian and write a caption telling about something they learned about the animal. Put the pictures in a folder in your science center for students to enjoy independently.

WRITING: A COMING-ALIVE STORY

Invite students to work in cooperative groups to write and illustrate an original story about a toy animal that comes alive, using *Alexander and the Wind-Up Mouse* as a model. As motivation, you might discuss other stories in which toys come alive or act alive, such as *The Velveteen Rabbit, Winnie-the-Pooh, The Constant Tin Soldier,* or *The Nutcracker.* When they come alive, what do these toys do that nonliving things can't?

Suggest that each group choose a toy animal from the class collection to tell about in their story. Together, group members can decide on the plot of the story and the main steps in the plot. Then members can pair off, each partner team being responsible for drawing and writing about one of the plot steps. A group compiler can put the finished pages in story order, a group editor can suggest ways to make the writing clearer, and two group members can be responsible for designing a cover for the story. The group as a whole can decide how to publish its story for the class. Perhaps they'll want to act it out together. Or the group can appoint a reader or readers to share the book with the class.

As a culminating activity, discuss with the class whether the finished stories belong in the class reading center or in the science center. Guide your students to understand that factual presentations are in the realm of science, while imagination and fantasy are in the realm of literature.

TECHNOLOGY: HOW THINGS MOVE

Use this activity to point out that movement alone does not prove something is alive. Initiate the activity by discussing things in the air and sky that move but are not alive: balloons, clouds, kites, and planes are examples. Invite volunteers to tell about the forces that move such things—the force of the wind, jet engines or propellers, and so on. Move on to a discussion of inanimate things that move over water (e.g., ships, canoes, paper boats, and water itself); and over land (e.g., trucks, cars, wagons, sleds, skates, etc.). Encourage students to discuss how movement is achieved for these inanimate things (e.g., wind in sails, oars, motors, the gravitational pull on water that makes it flow downhill, engines, wheels, blades, horsepower for the cart, etc.).

Next ask students to select a toy from the classroom collection and demonstrate and explain to classmates how it can be moved.

From *Science & Stories,* Grades K-3, published by GoodYearBooks. Copyright © 1994 Hilarie N. Staton and Tara McCarthy.

For example, a simple stuffed animal toy or model can be pushed across the floor by hand; a toy on a string moves when it's pulled. A battery-powered toy moves when you switch it on, and a wind-up toy moves when you turn the key. (The key winds up a spring inside, which, while unwinding, activates the toy to move.) Stress how all these movements emanate from forces implemented or invented by humans. As a culminating discussion, review why Willy, as a toy, can move only when a human turns his key and winds up his spring, and why Willy, as a real mouse, moves through his own energy.

Challenge interested students to bring in or describe other toys that move because of human force or technology. For example, some toys move toward light because of photoelectric cells, or respond to radio waves given off in a handset manipulated by a human.

ART: FABULOUS CRITTERS

Invite children to design and make imaginary animals out of scrap materials you provide: egg cartons, small milk cartons, pipe cleaners, scrap paper, buttons, wall-paper samples, sequins, and so on. Place these in a central work area, along with glue, scissors, pencils, and coloring materials. Encourage your artists to name their critters and make up details about where they live, how they grow, what they eat and drink, how they move, and how they take care of their young. After students have shown and discussed their fabulous critters, display them on a table or bookcase. Invite students to make up written or oral stories about the critters to share with the class.

APPLYING THE SCIENCE CONCEPT:

Invite students to do further research to find out more about real mice. Ask them to report to the class additional facts they've discovered. Suggested titles include:

"Mother Mouse," *Ranger Rick,* December, 1990.

Mousekin's Birth. Edna Miller. Prentice-Hall, 1974.

Nature encyclopedias and field guides

Alexander and the Wind-Up Mouse

Name _____ Date _____

Directions
Find and draw pictures of things that are living and nonliving.

MY FIELD TRIP RECORD

LIVING THINGS	NONLIVING THINGS
1. _____	1. _____
2. _____	2. _____
3. _____	3. _____
4. _____	4. _____
5. _____	5. _____
6. _____	6. _____

From *Science & Stories*, Grades K-3, published by GoodYearBooks. Copyright © 1994 Hilarie N. Staton and Tara McCarthy.

From *Science & Stories*, Grades K-3, published by GoodYearBooks. Copyright © 1994 Hilarie N. Staton and Tara McCarthy.

LESSON 7

LITERATURE:
The Very Hungry Caterpillar
Eric Carle (Philomel, 1987)

SCIENCE:
Patterns of Change

UNDERSTANDING:
Animals go through stages of development.

INQUIRY SKILLS:
Observing, predicting, revising data

AHEAD of TIME

WHAT YOU'LL NEED

For Building the Science Connection (for each pair of students)

- an open shoe box containing three or four mealworms
- apple slices
- dry oatmeal
- copies of Activity Sheet 7 for recording observations

For Follow-Up Activities:

- tagboard cutouts of what the caterpillar eats: 1 apple, 2 pears, 3 plums, 4 strawberries, and 5 oranges. Make a hole in each fruit large enough for a child to slip a hand through. See the book illustrations for models. (Oral Language)
- tagboard for book covers (Writing)
- picture of monarch butterfly (Geography/Ecology)
- enlarged map showing habitats and migrations of monarchs (Geography/Ecology)

STORY SUMMARY

The story takes our hero through his four stages of development: egg, caterpillar, pupa (or cocoon/chrysalis), and butterfly. Fantasy and fun enter this story at the caterpillar stage: in real life, caterpillars feed voraciously on green leaves. This caterpillar eats the fruits named above in Ahead of Time, plus a wide variety of other things, such as cake, pickles, ice cream, and sausage. This diet—bizarre for a caterpillar!—earns him a stomachache, which is relieved when he starts to eat his natural food, leaves. When he grows fat, he goes into his third, pupal stage and later emerges as a beautiful butterfly.

READING STRATEGIES

PRE-READING

Discuss animals whose young look like their parents (kittens, puppies, calves, ducklings, etc.). Talk about what these animals eat and why they need to eat (to live and grow). As you show the book cover and read the title, explain that the story is about an animal that has four different forms as it grows to adulthood. Call on volunteers to tell what they know about caterpillars. Prompt questions include: What does a caterpillar grow up to be? What does a caterpillar eat? On the chalkboard, list all of your students' ideas headed "What We Know About Caterpillars." Explain that students can change or add to the list after they finish listening to the story.

At this point, also, you may wish to set up the science investigation. Distribute the materials as listed in Ahead of Time. Explain that mealworms, like caterpillars, are insects. The mealworms will live and grow as long as they have appropriate food. They will go through the same stages of growth as the caterpillar. Ask partners to feed their mealworms apple slices and dry oatmeal. (Fresh apple slices can be added, but the oatmeal should be left undisturbed.)

WHILE READING

Ask students to listen for and find in the pictures the four different forms the animal takes: egg, caterpillar, pupa (cocoon), and butterfly. When you come to the "stomachache" part of the story, help children to see that the foods the caterpillar has been eating are not appropriate foods for this insect, and that he feels better when he starts to chomp on his natural food, leaves. Have children discuss and decide whether a real caterpillar would try to eat the fun things this storybook caterpillar eats. Conclude the story by inviting children to revise and add to their "What We Know About Caterpillars" list.

SCIENCE STRATEGIES

BUILDING THE SCIENCE CONNECTION

Distribute Activity Sheet 7 to the student partners and demonstrate how to use the sheets to draw pictures of how their mealworms grow and change.

Explain that the mealworms in the box were once eggs, as the Very Hungry Caterpillar once was. Ask students to draw a tiny egg in Box 1. In Box 2, ask students to draw their

mealworms as they are now. Explain that this is the *larval* stage, the same stage as The Very Hungry Caterpillar. Write "larva" on the chalkboard for children to copy on the Activity Sheet.

Allow a couple of minutes twice a day for partners to observe the development of the larvae as they eat the oatmeal and apples. The pupa stage is reached as the worm begins to turn into a beetle. When the animal becomes a full-fledged beetle, it is an adult. Write the words *pupa* and *adult* on the chalkboard for children to copy under their third and fourth drawings on their Activity Sheets.

Ask partners to show their completed Activity Sheets and tell in sequence what each drawing shows. Discuss how food is vital if the insect is to live and grow in the way the children have shown. Invite students to compare each stage of their mealworms with the stages of growth of The Very Hungry Caterpillar and to contrast the foods the different insects eat—leaves for the caterpillar, apples and oatmeal for the mealworms.

Conclude the activity by having a Free the Beetles celebration. On a mild day, children can release their beetles outdoors in a field or park. As partners free their beetles, suggest that they say a thank-you to or a special wish for these animals—who have, after all, helped your students to learn something important about living things.

EXTENDING THE SCIENCE CONNECTION

Activity 1. Make a companion chart to "What We Know About Caterpillars," heading it "What We Want to Find Out About Caterpillars." After discussing how some caterpillars change into butterflies while others change into moths, invite the class to brainstorm some questions about moths and butterflies.

From *Science & Stories, Grades K–3,* published by GoodYearBooks. Copyright © 1994 Hilarie N. Staton and Tara McCarthy.

Activity 2. Encourage a small group of interested students to use encyclopedias and nonfiction library books to find the differences between these insects. Ask them to look also for facts about what adult butterflies or moths feed upon. Suggest that they present their findings as an oral report with pictures.

Activity 3. Invite K–1 students to discuss other insects they know about, such as ants, bees, grasshoppers, and dragonflies. Emphasize that we usually see these insects in their adult stage. Invite students to predict the first three stages of these insects (egg, larva, pupa).

FOLLOW-UP ACTIVITIES

ORAL LANGUAGE: RETELLING THE STORY IN SEQUENCE

Use the big cutouts you've prepared (see Ahead of Time) and work with a small group of students. Invite one student to stand beside you and play the part of the Very Hungry Caterpillar as you retell the story. Ask other group members to follow along in the book. As you come to the part of the story in which the caterpillar begins to eat the fruits, ask your audience to tell which fruit the caterpillar eats first, second, third, and so forth. Ask the caterpillar-actor to slip her or his hand through the hole in the fruit to demonstrate the action as you tell that part of the story. Since this is an acting role that children love, you may find yourself repeating the retelling with other "caterpillars."

As a related art and drama activity, invite interested students to make big cutouts of the other things the caterpillar eats (cake, ice cream cone, pickle, and finally a leaf). Then use all the cutouts to act out the story in sequence for the whole class or for a group of classmates.

WRITING: THE VERY HUNGRY MEALWORM

Invite students to work in groups to write and illustrate a story about their mealworms, using *The Very Hungry Caterpillar* as a model. To

begin, the group as a whole can discuss their completed Activity Sheets to review the four stages the mealworm goes through. Suggest that the group then brainstorm a list of fantastic foods the mealworm might try before it settles down to a sensible diet of apples and oatmeal. The group can appoint a scribe to write down their food ideas. After that, other roles can be assigned. For example, two group members can write and illustrate pages about the mealworm as an egg hatching into a worm. Individual group members can make cutout pages showing silly foods the mealworm tries. Two group members can make cutout pages showing the mealworm finally dining on apples and oatmeal. Assign one group member to illustrate the very hungry mealworm in its pupa stage. Another group member can illustrate the insect in its adult beetle stage.

Suggest that each group write or dictate to you captions for each story picture. Have the group assemble the story pages into a book. Provide oaktag or construction paper to use as a book cover. After the groups' designated spokespersons have shown the books to the class, put the books in your science center for students to read and discuss on their own.

GEOGRAPHY/ECOLOGY: MAPPING THE MONARCHS

To help students develop the concept that some butterflies, like some birds, migrate between summer and winter habitats in order to find food, display an enlargement of the following map. Show a picture of a monarch butterfly. Explain how the map and the color key show where monarchs spend the summer, the migration path they take as cool weather sets in, and the regions where they winter. Orient your students to the map by asking them to designate the same areas on your wall map of North America and asking where they would go to see monarch butterflies at different times of the year. Invite interested students to use encyclopedias and periodicals (for example, the October, 1991 issue of *Ranger Rick*) to find out about the specific foods monarchs need, the reasons these food sources are dwindling, the effect on the monarch population, and what concerned people are doing to try to assure the monarch's survival.

APPLYING THE SCIENCE CONCEPT:

☑ Ask student partners to make menus for a make-believe Living Things Diner. Suggest they line up at least three different meals for three different kinds of animals, at least one of which should be healthy food for the caterpillar or mealworm. Encourage children to include a healthy meal for themselves. Invite students to show and discuss their menus after your class snack time.

Summer Range

Wintering Sites

Migration Routes

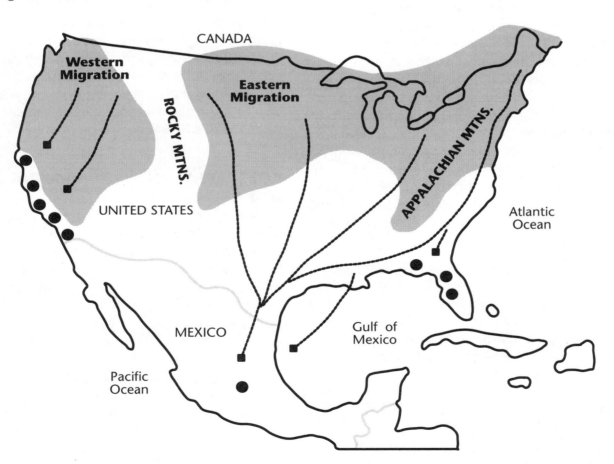

Butterfly Migration Map from ZOOBOOKS: *Butterflies.* Copyright © 1990 by Wildlife Education, Ltd. Reprinted by permission.

From *Science & Stories*, Grades K–3, published by GoodYearBooks. Copyright © 1994 Hilarie N. Staton and Tara McCarthy.

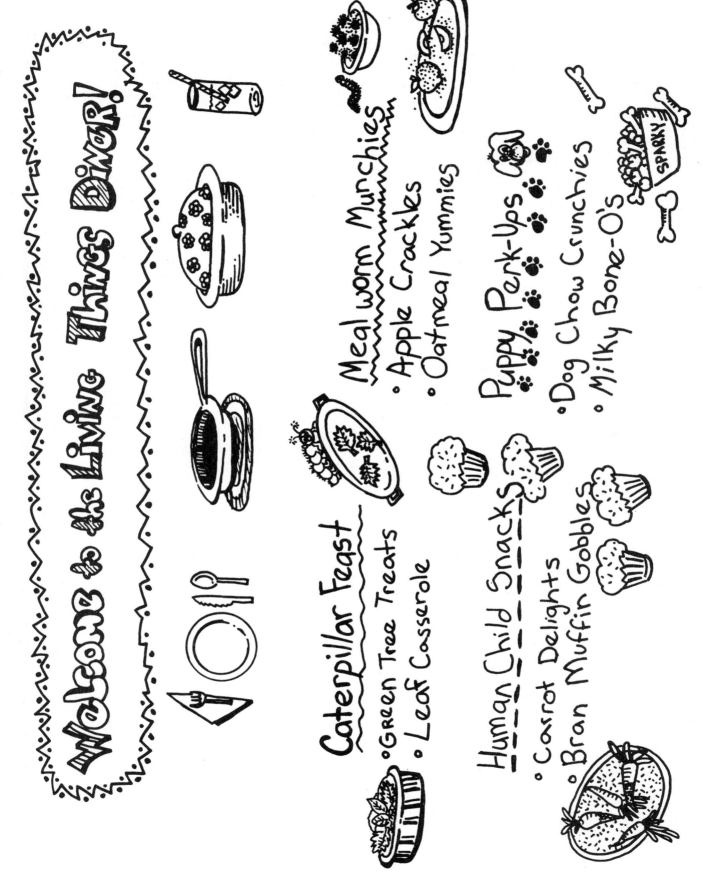

Welcome to the Living Things Diner!

Mealworm Munchies
- Apple Crackles
- Oatmeal Yummies

Puppy Perk-Ups
- Dog Chow Crunchies
- Milky Bone-O's

Caterpillar Feast
- Green Tree Treats
- Leaf Casserole

Human Child Snacks
- Carrot Delights
- Bran Muffin Gobbles

The Very Hungry Caterpillar

Name _____ Date _____

HOW OUR MEALWORMS GROW AND CHANGE

Directions
Listen to the directions your teacher gives you.

1. egg	**2.**
3.	**4.**

What did the mealworms eat? Draw pictures to show the food.

From *Science & Stories*, Grades K-3, published by GoodYearBooks. Copyright © 1994 Hilarie N. Staton and Tara McCarthy.

LESSON 8

LITERATURE:
The Mixed-Up Chameleon
Eric Carle (Harper, 1984)

SCIENCE:
Scale and Structure

UNDERSTANDING:
Living things have properties that enable them to survive.

INQUIRY SKILLS:
Observing, identifying variables, recording data, interpreting data, generalizing

AHEAD of TIME

WHAT YOU'LL NEED

For Building the Science Connection
• an aquarium with three different kinds of fish: a bottom-feeder, such as a catfish; a fish that swims in the middle of the aquarium, such as a goldfish; a fish that darts to the top of the water to get food, such as a sunfish

For Extending the Science Connection
• Nonfiction books and junior nature encyclopedias or periodicals that show some of the animals in the story getting food. For example, find articles that show giraffes and elephants reaching for leaves on trees, seals catching fish, polar bears catching seals, deer grazing, or turtles snapping at bugs.
• art materials

For Follow-Up Activities
• small pictures of different animals (Oral Language)
• bag or box to hold pictures (Oral Language)

STORY SUMMARY
The chameleon has characteristics that make it very special: it can change color, and it has a long, sticky tongue that can dart out to catch bugs, its primary food. But this chameleon wishes to look like and act like other animals it sees at a zoo. As its wishes comes true, the chameleon acquires structures such as the wings of a flamingo, the whiteness of a polar bear, the tail of a fox, and the long neck of a giraffe. In getting all these structures, the mixed-up chameleon is unable to catch its favorite food, a fly. So the chameleon wishes to just be itself again. That wish granted, the chameleon returns to its original structure and is able to zap up the fly.

READING STRATEGIES
PRE-READING
As you show the book cover, explain that a chameleon is a kind of lizard that lives in trees and bushes and eats insects. Invite students to find the chameleon's tongue in the cover picture. Explain that the tongue is very long and very sticky, and that the chameleon can scoot

fast over leaves and dart its tongue out quickly to catch a bug to eat. You might also wish to tell about other characteristics. For example, some chameleons are very small (about 1¼ " long) and some are larger (25" long). Chameleons change color when the light or temperature changes, or when they are frightened. As they change colors, chameleons blend with their surroundings. A chameleon might look green on a green leaf, gray in a shadow, or reddish on a red flower petal. As a preview to the story theme (wishing to be different), ask students if they would like being able to change to many different colors. Ask students to explain why or why not. Ask students to listen to the story to find out what the chameleon wishes and why it gets mixed up.

WHILE READING

Use the thumb index on the left-hand pages to help students keep track of the animals the chameleon admires, and to guide them as they point to the structures the chameleon acquires as its wishes are granted. Using the thumb index and the big illustrations as a sequencing activity, invite children to retell each page as a cumulative story; for example: "Now the chameleon has the color of a polar bear, the wings and legs of a flamingo, and a fox's tail." "Next it has the color of a polar bear, the wings and legs of a flamingo, a fox's tail, and a fish's fins." As the chameleon gets more and more mixed-up and acquires slower moving feet and an elephant's head, ask "Do you think the chameleon might have trouble catching a fly now? Why?" Before turning to the last page of the story, invite students to predict what the chameleon will wish last.

SCIENCE STRATEGIES
BUILDING THE SCIENCE CONNECTION

Introduce the activity by reviewing what the chameleon eats and how it catches its food. Briefly discuss what students know about what other animals eat and how they get food. Then explain that this investigation will help them discover how some kinds of fish get food. Ask children to form groups of four or five. Explain that the groups will observe the fish in the aquarium to see how they get food. Identify the fish in the tank and write catfish, goldfish, and sunfish on the chalkboard. Distribute Activity Sheet 8 to each student and explain that group members will use it to record their observations over a three-day period. (Set aside about ten minutes on each of the three days for groups to feed the fish and make their observations.)

Ask the groups to assign roles. For example, one member of each group can feed the fish. The feeders from different groups can rotate this assignment or carry it out together. Caution the feeders not to overfeed their fish, for this will make the tank dirty and kill the fish. All group members should observe and discuss "who eats where" in the tank as they watch the fish take in the food during each feeding period. Two members can collate the group's observations on the first day by indicating where to draw the specific fish on the Activity Sheet. Two other members can tell where the same fish feed on the second and third days of observation. These members can help others in the group put check marks in the correct places on their Activity Sheet.

Your students will find that the catfish swims slowly along the bottom of the tank to pick up food. The goldfish generally stays at midlevel to catch food drifting down, and the sunfish darts to the top to snatch the food on the surface.

Conclude the activity by inviting students to look closely at the catfish and describe how its physical structure allows it to get food as it does. Catfish have mouths on their undersides and long feelers to help them search out food in the corners and crevices at the bottom of the tank.

Discuss how goldfish and sunfish don't have these structures. Invite interested students to do some research on sunfish and goldfish. Find out what structures they have that enable them to

From *Science & Stories*, Grades K-3, published by GoodYearBooks. Copyright © 1994 Hilarie N. Staton and Tara McCarthy.

get food at their special levels in the water.

Finally, ask what would happen if the mixed-up chameleon wished for and got the mouth and whiskers of a catfish. Would he have a hard time catching a fly? Why?

EXTENDING THE SCIENCE CONNECTION

Activity 1. Second- and third-grade students can use library books and reference books you've provided to find out about structures and behaviors that enable different animals to get food. For example, giraffes with their long necks and elephants with their long trunks can reach up high to get leaves to eat. Seals have flippers that enable them to swim swiftly to chase and catch their food, fish.

Activity 2. Invite students to choose two of the animals the mixed-up chameleon admires. Ask them to draw pictures of the two animals getting their food, and present the pictures to the class. Then help students write captions for their pictures. Display the finished work around the room or put it in a folder in your science center for students to read and talk about independently.

FOLLOW-UP ACTIVITIES

ORAL LANGUAGE: ACTING OUT THE STORY THEME

Put lots of pictures of different animals into a box or bag. Have a small group of students sit in a circle around you. Ask each student in turn to say "I wish I were a . . . ," then reach in for a picture at random, name the animal (". . .a bear!"), and show the picture to the other players. Encourage players to ask questions of the "bear," such as "How do you move?" "Where do you live?" "What do you eat?" "How do you get your food?" Ask your actor to act out or say the responses, with you and other players helping along the way with hints when necessary. Bring down the curtain on each mini-performance by asking the actor: "What can a (bear) do that you can't do? What can **you** do that a (bear) can't do?"

WRITING: A THUMB INDEX BOOK ABOUT ANIMALS

Invite students to work in groups to make a book about animals that is thumb-indexed like *The Mixed-Up Chameleon.* Introduce the activity by starting at the back of the book and giving an example of how you can use the index. For instance: "I want to find out how the chameleon looks when it gets a deer's antlers. So I'll just put my thumb right here on the little picture of the deer and open to that page, and there it is!" After students have practiced the strategy a few times, they are ready to work in their groups and assign roles. In a central location, supply heavy paper or tagboard, rulers, scissors, crayons, pencils, colored markers, and binding materials (tape, yarn, hole-punchers, staplers).

The whole group can brainstorm exactly what they want their animal book to show. Examples include baby animals, animals getting food, places where animals live, animals in our area, pet animals, and wild animals. The whole group should also decide how many animal pages they want their book to have and the sequence in which the animals will appear in the book. (Encourage your writers to have no more than eight animals.)

Divide the tasks of assembling the book among the members of each group. One group member can act as scribe and make a sequential picture list of the animals. Two other group members can measure and cut out the pages to allow for thumb indexing in each one. Suggest that they use the pages in *The Mixed-Up Chameleon* as a guide for measuring and cutting pages.

Each group member can then be responsible for completing a page of the book. The full page shows that animal in whatever theme the group has decided upon. A small picture of the animal goes on the thumb-index part. While one group member puts the thumb indexed pages in sequence, two other group members can make and illustrate a back and front cover for the book. The back cover might list the names of the contributors. One or two members can bind the final book for presentation to the class. After group spokespersons have shown the books to the class and students have discussed them, put the books on a table in your science center where your students can read them.

MATH: CHAMELEON PROBLEMS

Invite interested students to make up and present to a group of classmates funny math word problems based on ideas from *The Mixed-Up Chameleon.* Examples: (a) The chameleon has four legs. If he gets two more legs from a bird, and four more legs from a deer, how many legs will he have altogether? (b) The chameleon has no wings. If he gets two wings from a bat, how many wings will he have? After students respond correctly to the problems, they may wish to prove their answers by drawing pictures.

ART: CUT-PAPER CREATURES

In a central work area, supply students with construction-paper scraps, scissors, paste, markers, and big sheets of heavy paper for backing. Introduce the activity by reviewing the pictures in the book and talking about all the "attachments" the chameleon accumulates. Invite students to use the art materials to make their own mixed-up creatures. Encourage students to invent names for their fantastic animals. Some students may also wish to write captions describing where their fantastic creatures live, what they eat, and how they get their food. Display the finished work around the room. Suggest that individual students or partners make up stories about the animals to share with the class.

APPLYING THE SCIENCE CONCEPT:

☑ Ask student partners to make a picture chart of what human beings eat and how they get their food. You might refer third-grade students to Joanna Cole's *The Magic School Bus Inside the Human Body* (page 105) to find facts about how food is used and processed within our bodies.

From *Science & Stories, Grades K–3,* published by GoodYearBooks. Copyright © 1994 Hilarie N. Staton and Tara McCarthy.

The Mixed-Up Chameleon

Name _____ Date _____

WHERE OUR FISH EAT

DIRECTIONS
Watch the fish for three days. Draw pictures to show where they are in the tank each day.

DAY 1

Fish at the top:

_____

Fish in the middle:

_____

Fish at the bottom:

_____

No Fishing Allowed

DAY 2

Fish at the top:

_____

Fish in the middle:

_____

Fish at the bottom:

_____

DAY 3

Fish at the top:

_____

Fish in the middle:

_____

Fish at the bottom:

_____

LITERATURE:
Ox-Cart Man
Donald Hall (Puffin, 1979)

SCIENCE:
Systems and Interactions

UNDERSTANDING:
The sun is a source of heat energy.

INQUIRY SKILLS:
Observing, interpreting data, predicting

AHEAD (of) TIME

WHAT YOU'LL NEED

For Building the Science Connection
- two large, clear glasses
- ice cubes
- a place where you can put one glass in direct sun and the other in shade

For Extending the Science Connection
- a globe (on its axis)
- a red sticker or wax pencil to mark the North Pole on the globe
- a green sticker to mark your region on the globe
- a bright table lamp or floor lamp

For Follow-Up Activities
- four hats representing the four seasons: for example, a stocking cap (winter), a rain hat (spring), a straw hat (summer), and a felt hat (fall) (Oral Language)
- a large box to hold the hats (Oral Language)
- tape recorder (Writing)
- weather chart, weather symbols, and markers (Math)
- copies of Activity Sheet 9 (Applying the Science Concept)

STORY SUMMARY
The setting is the farmland around Portsmouth, New Hampshire, about 200 years ago. The story tells of the day-to-day activities of the ox-cart man and his family from fall through spring. In October, the family loads the ox-cart with all the surplus materials and goods they've produced throughout the year: wool and goose feathers, vegetables and fruits, mittens and shawls, shingles and birch brooms. The father takes these to Portsmouth and sells them, along with the ox and the cart. He returns home on foot, with some money and a few supplies he's bought in town. Through the winter and spring, the family works together to produce more things to use and sell.

READING STRATEGIES
PRE-READING
As you show the book cover, invite children to find a picture clue (the fallen leaves) to guess what season of the year it is (fall, autumn). On a globe, point out the general area of Portsmouth, New Hampshire, and explain that this is where the story takes place. Point out your area on the globe and ask children to tell about signs of fall there. Write the names of the

From *Science & Stories*, Grades K-3, published by GoodYearBooks. Copyright © 1994 Hilarie N. Staton and Tara McCarthy.

four seasons on the chalkboard. Invite children to listen to the story to find out what three seasons it tells about.

WHILE READING

Pause now and then in your reading to invite children to point out picture clues that tell about the changing seasons. These clues are best seen in the panoramic landscapes, the changing sky and foliage, and people's clothing. Weave temperature words (hot, cold, warm, chilly, etc.) into the discussion.

Conclude the reading by inviting children to name the seasons the book portrays (autumn, winter, spring), to predict the season that comes next, and to suggest what summer activities the ox-cart family will carry out (tending the crops, gathering feathers, making brooms, making candles, etc.). To lead into the Science Connections, you might ask "What will the temperature be like in summer? Will it be hotter or colder than it is in spring? Why do you think so?"

SCIENCE STRATEGIES
BUILDING THE SCIENCE CONNECTION

Invite volunteers to help you set up the investigation. Fill each glass with an equal number of ice cubes. Put one glass in direct sun and the other in the shade. Ask students to predict in which glass the ice cubes will melt more quickly. Then ask them to check their predictions by observing what happens.

Ask: "Which glass gets more of the sun's heat? What does the heat energy do to the ice cubes?" Build a link to the literature by inviting students to tell which glass reminds them of summer on the ox-cart farm, and which reminds them of winter. Ask children to decide in which season they feel the most heat from the sun.

EXTENDING THE SCIENCE CONNECTION

We experience seasons because the earth is tilted on its axis. To introduce this concept, invite children to carry out the following investigation: Set up the lamp in the center of the

Spring
Move the globe tipped this way.

Winter
Tilt the North Pole away from the sun.

Summer
Tilt the North Pole towards the sun.

Fall
Move the globe tipped this way.

demonstration area. Ask children to imagine that the lamp is the sun. Point out the North Pole and your region on the globe. Call on a volunteer to hold the globe and move it slowly around the sun, following your directions, which are suggested in italics in the diagram on the previous page. (Make sure the globe is close enough to the lamp to make a dramatic show of light. You might also turn off the lights and pull the shades to darken the room.)

Ask students to notice the tilt on the circling globe and to observe when your region (marked with the sticker) is tilted toward the sun and when it is tilted away from the sun. Encourage them to decide at which of these positions your part of earth is getting the most light and heat from the sun and when it is getting the least. Then discuss which tilt brings summer and which brings winter.

You may wish to review the landscapes in the book that show fall, winter, and spring. Then ask children to choose the picture that shows what happens when the ox-cart family's farm is tilted away from the sun. Discuss what a picture would show when the farm is most tilted toward the sun (a summer landscape).

Further Reading. K–1 children will enjoy listening to Debra Frasier's *On the Day You Were Born* and discussing the pictures that show earth, sun, moon, and the seasons. With children at higher reading and comprehension levels, read Terri Cholene's *Dancing Drum: A Cherokee Legend* and discuss what it tells about our dependence on the heat and light of the sun.

FOLLOW-UP ACTIVITIES

ORAL LANGUAGE: A HAT FOR EVERY SEASON!

For this small-group game, you'll need the four hats and large box listed in the Ahead of Time section. Introduce the game by reviewing the seasons, weather, and seasonal activities shown in the book illustrations. Invite children to discuss their own activities and surroundings at different seasons of the year.

Ask players to sit in a circle. Explain to them what season each hat stands for. Put the hats in the box. Play goes around the circle in turn. The first player reaches into the box, takes out a hat, puts it on, and announces what season he or she represents. The player then tells about something that happens in that season (e.g., "Snow is falling," or "I have to wear mittens," or "The ox-cart man is making a new cart.") If other players agree that the event fits the season, write the event on the chalkboard. Then it's the next player's turn to reach into the box, put on a hat, and tell about the season.

Continue play until each player has had at least two turns. Since a player can pick a hat by feeling it in the box, encourage her or him to choose a different season in each round. Also encourage players to come up with new ideas for each season, rather than repeating what another player has said. If a player gets stuck, encourage others in the group to help with suggestions.

Conclude the game by reading players' ideas from the chalkboard list, asking them to identify again the season each one tells about. Invite interested students to draw picture strips of themselves in their different hats at different seasons. Display the picture strips on a bulletin board or around the room.

WRITING: A CLASS "CATALOG POEM"

Several of the pages in *Ox-Cart Man* use clusters of repetitive sentences (e.g., sentences beginning with "He packed. . ." or "He bought. . ."). Such sentences can turn prose into "catalog poems." Briefly review these pages with the class. Then suggest that students work in four groups, each group writing a catalog poem about one of the seasons. Suggest that each line of the group's poem begin with the season's name ("Winter is. . .") or with the season's name and a sensory verb ("Winter tastes like . . .," "Winter smells like . . .").

Groups can assign roles to members. Each child should contribute at least one line to the poem. One or two members can act as group scribes and write the lines on scrap paper. (If possible, make a tape recorder available to each group; this will make the scribes' work faster and easier.) The scribe or another group member can write the final lines in "very best writing" on a sheet of poster paper. Ask the transcribers to leave space between or after each line for an illustration. Two or three group members can be assigned to illustrate.

A spokesperson can read and show the final poem to the class; or the group might practice and use choral reading, with group members taking turns reading some lines solo and others in unison. Have groups present their catalog poems in seasonal sequence; later, display them that way.

MATH: MEASURING THE SEASON

Invite interested students to form a "season-watcher" group to record weather data over a one- or two-week period. Supply the group with a weather chart, an outdoor thermometer, and a list of picture symbols. Have the students put the thermometer in a place that is away from direct sunlight. For each day on the chart, your "season-watchers" will record the temperature at two different times of day and draw the symbol or symbols that describe that day's weather. Keep the chart on display so that the entire class can watch it develop. Invite all students to comment about each day's weather. Is it just what they would expect at this season of the year, or is it unusual (e.g., a snowstorm in June)?

When the chart is completed, discuss with the class some generalizations about the season that might be based on the data. (These will vary, of course, from region to region.) You might also challenge your "season-watcher" group to find other data that meteorologists record, such as wind speed, rainfall or other precipitation, and the time of sunrise and sunset.

Enlist family helpers at home. Weather data is available in most daily newspapers and on early morning local radio and TV news broadcasts. Challenge interested students to figure out how sunrise and sunset times relate to the changing amount of sunlight their region is getting as the tilted earth moves around the sun.

APPLYING THE SCIENCE CONCEPT:

☑ Distribute Activity Sheet 9. Discuss the seasonal activities of the ox-cart family, as shown in the left column. For the right column, ask children to draw a picture of an activity they do or an object they use in that season. Ask children to cut the eight cards out and write the name of the appropriate season on the back.

Demonstrate one game that can be played with the cards. Put pairs of cards picture side up and challenge a partner to guess the season. Encourage partners and small groups to create and demonstrate other ways to use the cards in a game. For example, shuffle the cards picture side up and ask a partner to make season pairs. Or put the cards picture side down and challenge a partner to name two activities or objects associated with the season written on the back of the cards.

From *Science & Stories*, Grades K-3, published by GoodYearBooks. Copyright © 1994 Hilarie N. Staton and Tara McCarthy.

Ox-Cart Man

Name _____ Date _____

THE SEASONS

DIRECTIONS
For each season, draw a picture of something you do.

Winter

Spring

Summer

Fall

From *Science & Stories, Grades K-3*, published by GoodYearBooks. Copyright © 1994 Hilarie N. Staton and Tara McCarthy.

From *Science & Stories*, Grades K–3, published by GoodYearBooks. Copyright © 1994 Hilarie N. Staton and Tara McCarthy.

LITERATURE:
The Legend of the Bluebonnet
Tomie DePaola (Putnam, 1983)

SCIENCE:
Systems and Interactions

UNDERSTANDING:
Water evaporates when heat is applied.

INQUIRY SKILLS:
Observing, measuring, predicting, identifying variables, interpreting data

AHEAD of TIME

WHAT YOU'LL NEED

For Building the Science Connection
- saucer
- wax pencil
- water
- place outdoors where you can place the saucer for a few hours

For Extending the Science Connection
- spray bottle with a nozzle that adjusts to "fine" or "mist"
- large metal cookie sheet

For a Pre-Reading discussion, bring a potted flower to school.

For Follow-Up Activities (Writing):
- picture of your state flower
- pictures of other state symbols
- art materials for making books (construction paper, colored pencils or crayons, scissors, glue, paper punch, yarn or brads for binding pages)

STORY SUMMARY

The Comanche people are suffering from a long drought and famine. Their shaman explains that this is because the Great Spirits are offended; the people have taken much from the earth without giving anything back. To bring rain, the wise man says, the people must give back a valued possession by burning it in a fire. While the people believe their shaman, no adult steps forward to give anything up. That night, a young orphan girl, She-Who-Is-Alone, decides to sacrifice the thing she loves most; her doll, which is all she has left since her parents died. She goes alone to a hilltop, builds a fire, and sadly places her doll in it. When the ashes are cold, she scatters them to the Four Winds. The long-awaited rains come, and wherever the doll's ashes fall beautiful bluebonnets blossom. This, says the legend, is the origin of the bluebonnet, which blooms every spring in the land now known as Texas.

READING STRATEGIES
PRE-READING
Show the potted flower to the children and discuss what it needs in order to live and grow

(sun, air, water, soil). Focus on water by asking what would happen to the flower if no one watered it. As you show the book cover, discuss how dry the land looks in the picture. Then point out the pictures of the bluebonnets. Ask what will be needed to make these flowers grow on such dry land (water in the form of rain). Encourage children to predict what the story will tell about.

WHILE READING

Read the story straight through, but pause once or twice to make sure children understand why rain was necessary to the Comanche. The Comanche depend on buffalo and deer for food. These animals depend on grass to eat. Without rain, no grass or other plants will grow. So the animals die or go far away to find grazing land. Help children to define new story vocabulary, *drought* and *famine,* in this discussion context.

This story is extremely moving to many children because it involves giving up a beloved possession. After you finish reading the story, you might call on your students' ideas and insights from the discussion suggested above to help them clarify why She-Who-Is-Alone sacrificed a favorite possession. Elicit opinions about whether or not she did the right thing.

Encourage students to suggest other choices the heroine might have made and how she probably feels when the rain pours down and the bluebonnets and grass grow. Invite a volunteer to extend the story by telling what will happen now in the Comanche's land. (Game animals will return. People will have food to eat.)

SCIENCE STRATEGIES
BUILDING THE SCIENCE CONNECTION

Take the class outdoors on a dry, sunny day. Ask students to imagine that the saucer stands for She-Who-Is-Alone's land. Put water in the saucer and ask a student to draw a line around

the water with the wax pencil. Every two hours or so, trace the water level again. As children discuss the diminishing puddle, use the word *evaporate* to explain what is happening. The water evaporates, or turns into invisible water vapor that mixes with the air. Ask children to predict what will happen to the water in the saucer if no more water is added. (It will all evaporate, and the saucer will be dry.)

Discuss how the saucer would then be like the Comanche's land at the beginning of the story. For further practice with the inquiry skills, try the same investigation in a different weather condition so that your students can check the rate of evaporation. For example, water evaporates faster if the air is dry and if the weather is warm and windy. It evaporates more slowly if the air is moist and if the weather is cool and calm. Discuss what kind of weather might have caused the Comanche's land to dry up.

EXTENDING THE SCIENCE CONNECTION

To introduce the concept of how the invisible water vapor eventually becomes rain, explain first that the vapor from the saucer is rising into the air and that billions of such tiny invisible droplets eventually form clouds. Then invite volunteers to help you demonstrate what must happen next before the water vapor falls as rain.

Put the cookie sheet on end so that it stands straight against a wall. (If necessary, use small rocks or lumps of clay to brace the cookie sheet.) Ask children to imagine that the cookie sheet stands for a big cloud. Spray a fine mist of water on the cookie sheet several times. Ask children to observe what happens. (Some droplets cling to the surface.) Only when droplets blend together to make bigger drops does the water run down the cookie sheet. Ask "Which do you think are heavier—the tiny droplets or the big ones? Which drops fall— the heavy ones or the lighter ones? What must happen inside a cloud before the water vapor comes back to earth as raindrops?" (The drops

From *Science & Stories,* Grades K-3, published by GoodYearBooks. Copyright © 1994 Hilarie N. Staton and Tara McCarthy.

become so heavy that the cloud can no longer hold them, so they fall.)

Invite children to compare the legend in the story with their conclusions from this investigation. Ask them to give a "reason from science" and a "reason from legend" to explain why rain finally came to the dry land of the Comanche.

For reinforcement and extension of these concepts, you might wish to turn next to *Bringing the Rain to Kapiti Plain* (see Story 18).

FOLLOW-UP ACTIVITIES
ORAL LANGUAGE: NEW NAMES
Discuss the new name the Comanche gave to She-Who-Is-Alone (One-Who-Dearly-Loved-Her-People) and why this is an appropriate new name for her. Invite children to talk about new names they would like to have that tell about deeds or accomplishments they are proud of. For example, a child who is proud of having helped a friend find a lost mitten might want the name "He-Who-Is-Expert-at-Finding-Things." A child who especially loves math might choose "She-Who-Loves-Numbers." Write the new names on the chalkboard. Invite children to draw or paint self-portraits and label them with their new names. Display the pictures around the room. Suggest that students choose one of the portraits and make up a story about how the person acquired that name.

WRITING/SOCIAL STUDIES: STATE SYMBOL MINI-BOOKS
Introduce the activity by reviewing the story, explaining that the bluebonnet is now the official flower of Texas, and discussing why this is a good choice. (The flowers grow wild and in abundance in many parts of the state; the flower also commemorates the unselfish action of She-Who-Is-Alone.)

Invite children to work in cooperative learning groups of four or five to make minibooks that illustrate and label your state's official "living" symbols: flower, bird, and tree. (Some states also have official mammals and fish.) Then ask groups to make up a new state symbol. Display official symbols of your state in the classroom; and, if possible, bring in a real live sample of your state's flower. Show your state's flower and encourage children to describe it—its shape, color, size, fragrance, and places where they've seen it growing.

Discuss the other symbols in like fashion. Emphasize that state symbols are usually chosen because the thing portrayed is abundant in the state. Using this context of abundant, invite and list ideas for new and fanciful state symbols, such as a state cookie, a state sound, a state game or sport, a state snake, or a state weather condition.

Distribute art materials to each group and suggest roles. For example, each group member can draw an existing official symbol and label it. One group member can design and make a cover for the minibook. Then the group can come together again to choose a new symbol, such as one for a state sport. The group can assign two members to draw and label the new symbol, and two members to write a sentence or two about why this symbol is a good one for your state. Suggest that the group appoint a member to make a cover or folder for the symbols, and a spokesperson to show and share the minibook with the class. Save the new symbol for last, as a surprise. Invite the audience to tell what they like best about the new symbol. Place the minibooks on a reading table for students to enjoy and discuss with a partner.

As a follow-up, suggest that group members or their classmates make up oral legends to tell how the new symbol came to be. For example, if the group has chosen a state mammal, such as a bear, the legend might tell how a bear once led a child to a hilltop covered with berries, or helped the child find her or his way home.

ART/VOCABULARY: PICTURES OF WORDS

Brainstorm a chalkboard list of words that describes the Comanche's land before She-Who-Is-Alone brings the rain (for example, dry, hard, brown, dead, windy); and then after the rain comes (for example, green, alive, colorful, soft, wet). Help children add to the list of weather words, based on their own observations in their area (for example, sunny, cold, foggy, hot, stormy). Then demonstrate how many descriptive words can be written so that they show their meanings. Here are four examples:

Invite your students to write and color words from the list to show what each word means or what it feels like. After children have shared their picture words, you might put them in a "Weather Words" folder. Every day, ask a student to find and post the words that describe today's weather.

APPLYING THE SCIENCE CONCEPT:

☑ Distribute Activity Sheet 10. Explain that the picture tells about the water cycle (heat, water, rain), and the story they have read. Invite children to identify the five picture elements in sequence: (1) a lake, (2) water vapor, (3) clouds, (4) raindrops, and (5) bluebonnets. Write the terms on the chalkboard and ask children to write each one correctly in labels for the Activity Sheet picture. After children draw their pictures of She-Who-Is-Alone, invite them to share their work and explain why the heroine feels the way she does.

The Legend of the Bluebonnet

Name _____ Date _____

RAIN FOR THE BLUEBONNETS

DIRECTIONS
Follow the directions
your teacher gives you.

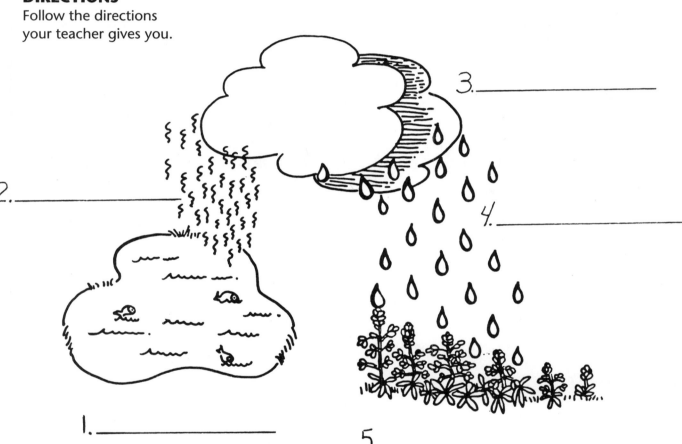

3. _____

2. _____

4. _____

1. _____

5. _____

How does She-Who-Is-Alone feel when the rain falls?
Finish the picture. Then cut it out and paste it on
the diagram above.

51

LITERATURE:
Time of Wonder
Robert McCloskey (Puffin, 1985)

SCIENCE:
Systems and Interactions

UNDERSTANDING:
Wind is air that is moving from place to place.

INQUIRY SKILLS:
Observing, interpreting data, recording data, manipulating materials

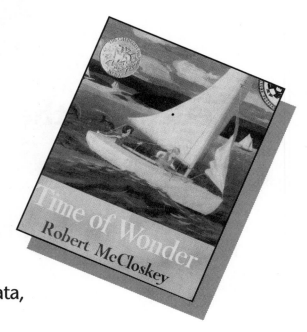

From *Science & Stories*, Grades K–3, published by GoodYearBooks. Copyright © 1994 Hilarie N. Staton and Tara McCarthy.

AHEAD *of* TIME

WHAT YOU'LL NEED

For Building the Science Connection
- an outdoor space, well away from buildings
- compass (or a large compass traced with chalk or drawn on tagboard and oriented toward true North)
- three or four outdoor sessions, on days when the wind is blowing from different directions and/or blows at markedly different wind speeds
- balloons on strings

For Extending the Science Connection
- small round mirror
- cardboard
- paste or glue
- dime-sized paper circle
- a marker, a compass, and a clear day with high white clouds

For Follow-Up Activities
- copies of wind speed chart on page 55
- recordings of music that evokes storms (Music/Art)
- art materials for making pictures that evoke storms—dark blue, purple, and gray construction paper; crayons; silver paper or aluminum foil for lightning bolt; cotton balls to shred for clouds (Music/Art)
- art materials for making Wind Whirls—scissors, crayons, lengths of yarn, yarn needles (Applying the Science Concept)

STORY SUMMARY

This is a lyrical description of a child's summer activities and observations at the Maine seashore. The mists and fogs of spring give way to the heat and sun of summer. Warm winds push clouds through the sky and fill the sails of boats. As fall approaches, so does a big wind—a hurricane—and people scamper about to batten down the hatches and prepare for it. After the storm comes calmer, cooler weather. In these last days of summer the children make their final explorations, then say goodbye to the sea until next year.

READING STRATEGIES

PRE-READING

As you share the book cover, discuss picture clues that show what the weather is like. How do you know it's warm? sunny? windy? Call attention to the way the wind fills the sails of the boat and makes waves in the water. Explain that the story is about a summer vacation and ask students to decide where the vacation takes place (seashore, ocean, beach). You might want to discuss the word *wonder* as it's used here to mean "surprise" or "delight." Invite children to predict what will be wonderful about the seashore vacation.

WHILE READING

You can use the story as an opportunity to build students' vocabulary of sensory words and phrases. Invite children to listen for words and phrases that they like a lot, or that are new to them. Pause after every two or three pages to collect and discuss your listeners' word finds. Write their contributions on the chalkboard or on poster paper. (You'll use this list in the Oral Language activity.) Examples are: *spill down* (for the rain), *fog turns yellow, light crisp feeling, heavy stillness, the scream of the wind.* As another vocabulary adventure, discuss *wonder* as it is used on the last page of the story: "to be curious about."

BUILDING THE SCIENCE CONNECTION

Review the book illustrations that show the effects of wind. Examples are on pages 6–9 (clouds moving closer and closer), 18–19 (tree limbs swaying), 20–21 (sailboats moving and waves kicking up), and 44–47 (effects of hurricane winds). Invite children to come outside to find out about the wind today.

Outdoors, explain to children that they will use the compass and the balloons to find out which direction the moving air, or wind, is coming *from*. (If necessary, review what N, S, E, and W stand for on the compass.) Hand out the balloons, and ask children to stand with them around the compass. As the balloons tilt in a general direction, such as south, challenge children to refer to the compass to decide where the wind is coming from (in this example, north) to push the balloons. Explain that this is called a *north wind.* Encourage children to describe the force of the wind: is it gentle? strong? Does it stop and start, or is it steady? Suggest that students make graphs to record their observations.

Repeat the investigation on two or three days when wind direction or force has changed. Back in the classroom, review some of the different wind conditions described in the book. Is the air always still in the story? Is the air always still in your area? Does it blow in from different directions? How do you know?

EXTENDING THE SCIENCE CONNECTION

Buildings and trees can influence and obstruct the path of moving air masses (wind). To get a more accurate account of which way the air is moving, interested students can make and use a nephoscope, or cloud indicator. (For materials and observation conditions, see Ahead of Time.)

Follow these construction steps. (1) Glue the mirror at the center of the cardboard; (2) Mark the compass points on the cardboard, around the mirror; (3) Paste the paper circle in the center of the mirror.

Here are the observation procedures. (1) Put the nephoscope outdoors, with N oriented toward true North; (2) Ask a student to look down into the mirror while a cloud passes over the paper circle in the center. Tell the student to follow the cloud's reflection until it reaches the edge of the mirror. At that point, the student will see a compass direction marked on the cardboard. Explain that this is the direction *toward* which the wind is blowing the cloud; (3) Remind students that winds are named for the direction *from* which they come.

Ask students to name the wind in this observation. It's the opposite of the direction of the cloud's movement. For example, if the cloud is drifting east, the wind is a west wind.

Back in the classroom, review page 32 in the story and discuss what the characters are probably observing as they make their weather predictions (direction in which the clouds are moving).

FOLLOW-UP ACTIVITIES

ORAL LANGUAGE: WEATHER IMAGERY

You can use the word and phrase list you made during the While Reading activity to spark a class brainstorming session about today's weather. Then ask children to take turns giving oral weather reports. Introduce the activity by reading and discussing the items on the list and inviting children to identify those that tell about wind and other weather conditions. Then call on children to think up words and phrases that describe today's weather in your area. Help children focus on the sun and its heat, the way the air feels (damp, dry), or any precipitation taking place, and the direction and speed of the wind. Encourage vivid descriptions and imagery. ("The wind is as soft as a baby's hair."; "The clouds are rushing like they're late to cloud-school.") Write children's descriptions on the chalkboard under column headings: Sun and Heat, Wind, Moisture. Call on volunteers to use descriptions from different columns as they give a complete weather report. Conclude the activi-ty by suggesting that children draw and label a picture of today's weather.

WRITING: WONDER BOOKS

Cooperative learning groups can make illus-trated "We Wonder" books that pose and illus-trate questions they have about weather and related phenomena. Introduce the activity by reviewing the last page of the story to find what the narrator wonders: "Where do hum-mingbirds go in a hurricane?" Brainstorm for questions your students have about the weath-er described in the book.

Ask groups to form questions about weather in their area or in a place they have visited or read about. Each group member can be responsible for writing one question on scrap paper. Two members can act as editors to check the questions for clarity. Each member then copies a question and illustrates it for a Wonder Book page. Suggest that the group assign members to make a book cover, to illus-trate it on the front, and to list contributors' names on the back. While these assignments are being carried out, two group members can make a final page for the book, headed How to Find Answers. Suggest that these partners talk to partners from other groups to get ideas. (For example, students can find answers by reading books, magazines, or encyclopedias; by looking at videos; by looking and listening; and by ask-ing someone who knows.)

After groups have shown and shared their Wonder Books with the class, put the books on a reading table for children to enjoy independ-ently or with reading partners.

MATH: FILLING IN A WIND SPEED CHART

This activity will help children put numbers in order and help them to understand that meteorologists use precise terms to describe weather phenomena. Prepare for the activity by making copies of the chart shown here. On the

From *Science & Stories*, Grades K-3, published by GoodYearBooks. Copyright © 1994 Hilarie N. Staton and Tara McCarthy.

chalkboard, list miles per hour in random order: 39–46, 4–7, 19–24, 47–54, 8–12, 32–38, 13–18, 55–63, 25–31.

Name of Wind	Miles Per Hour
Calm	Less than 1
Light Air	1–3
Light Breeze	
Gentle Breeze	
Moderate Breeze	
Fresh Breeze	
Strong Breeze	
Moderate Gale	
Fresh Gale	
Strong Gale	
Full Gale	
Violent Storm	64–75
Hurricane	Over 75

Discuss with students the clues in the second column that show how the wind scale is organized. Then challenge them to find the wind speed that goes with light breeze in the first column (4–7). Once you're pretty sure your math buffs have the hang of it, ask them to complete the chart independently or with partners, then check their charts with other participants. After reviewing the wind names, suggest that children make up questions for one another based on the chart. For example: "The wind is blowing at nine miles per hour. Name the wind." (gentle breeze) "There's a moderate gale coming our way. How fast will the wind be blowing?" (32 to 38 miles per hour).

The chart above is drawn from the Beaufort Scale, which is given in its entirety below. You might want to share the information in the Observation column with your students. Then have them observe the effects of today's wind and hypothesize what the name of the wind is.

The Beaufort Scale of the Speed of Wind

Scale Number	Observation	Name of Wind	Miles per Hour
0	Smoke goes straight up	Calm	Less than 1
1	Direction shown by smoke but not by wind vanes	Light Air	1-3
2	Wind vane moves; leaves rustle	Light Breeze	4-7
3	Flag flutters; leaves move constantly	Gentle Breeze	8-12
4	Raises dirt, paper; flags flap	Moderate Breeze	13-18
5	Small trees sway; flags ripple	Fresh Breeze	19-24
6	Large branches move; flags beat	Strong Breeze	25-31
7	Whole trees sway; flags are extended	Moderate Gale	32-38
8	Twigs break off; hard to walk against	Fresh Gale	39-46
9	Slight damage to buildings	Strong Gale	47-54
10	Trees uprooted; windows break	Full Gale	55-63
11	Widespread damage to buildings	Violent Storm	64-75
12	General destruction	Hurricane	Over 75

MUSIC/ART: STORMY SOUNDS

Review the pictures in the book that show the hurricane hitting sea and land. Distribute art materials and play some "stormy music." Suggested selections, all readily available on tape or CDs, include Claude Debussy's *La Mer,* "The Dialogue of the Wind and the Waves;" from Ludwig van Beethoven's *Fourth Symphony* (The "Pastoral"), the fourth movement, "Storm," and Modeste Mussorgsky's *Night on Bald Mountain.* Invite children to paint pictures of the weather scene they see in their mind's eye as they listen.

As children share their finished pictures, invite them to tell what colors and shapes they used to match the sounds in the music.

APPLYING THE SCIENCE CONCEPT:

Distribute Activity Sheet 11. Children can use their Wind Whirls to discover that we feel wind when hot air is rising. To begin the activity, demonstrate how to cut out the entire Wind Whirl, and then color it on both sides. Next show children how to cut along the guide lines to make the whirl. Help children use the needle to pull the yarn through the two holes and make a knot. (The yarn should not be twisted.)

Ask children to hold their Wind Whirls above sources of heat and cold to see when the Wind Whirl moves. (You'll have to supervise this carefully for safety's sake.) Heat sources can be a pail of hot water, a radiator, or an exposed lightbulb. Sources of cold can be an open window or a pail of icy water.

Children will notice that the Whirl moves most noticeably above heat sources, because hot air rises. Cold air sinks, so the Wind Whirl doesn't whirl when held above the source of cold.

☑ Encourage your students to extrapolate from this investigation to figure out when we feel wind (when hot air is rising).

From *Science & Stories,* Grades K-3, published by GoodYearBooks. Copyright © 1994 Hilarie N. Staton and Tara McCarthy.

Time of Wonder

Name _____ Date _____

WIND WHIRL

DIRECTIONS
Follow your teacher's directions to make your Wind Whirl.

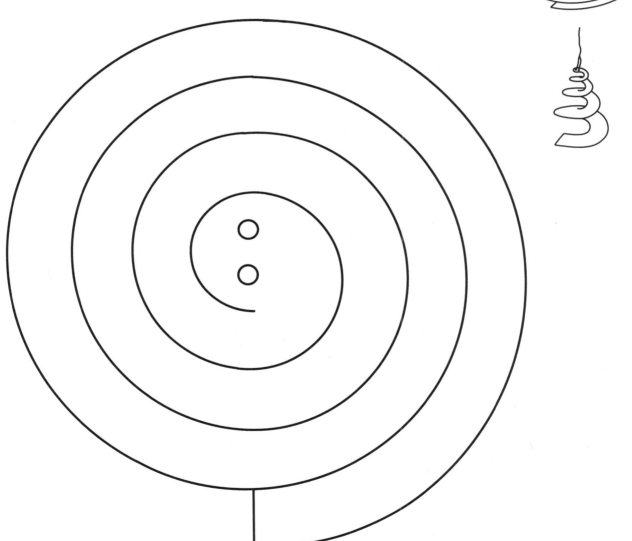

From BRAIN WAVES: *Weather Investigations* by Frances Ralph. Copyright © 1991 by Folens Limted. Reprinted by permission.

LITERATURE:
The Nightgown of the Sullen Moon
Nancy Willard (Harcourt, 1983)

SCIENCE:
Systems and Interactions

UNDERSTANDING:
The moon moves in orbit around the earth.
The earth and moon orbit the sun.

INQUIRY SKILLS:
Observing, predicting

From *Science & Stories*, Grades K-3, published by GoodYearBooks. Copyright © 1994 Hilarie N. Staton and Tara McCarthy.

AHEAD *of* TIME

WHAT YOU'LL NEED

For Building the Science Connection
- three balls of different sizes, such as a kickball, a tennis ball, and a table tennis ball
- small colored stickers
- a globe

For Follow-Up Activities
- art materials for making moon gowns—old sheets or white curtains, fabric and regular crayons, washable markers, scissors, scraps of construction paper and aluminum foil, paste, paper punch, yarn, yarn needles (Oral Language/Art/Drama)
- art materials for making pictures of moon gifts—construction paper, crayons, markers (Writing)
- art materials for drawing maps—construction paper, crayons, colored pencils, or markers (Geography)
- crayons, colored pencils, or markers for coloring Activity Sheet 12 (Applying the Science Connection)

STORY SUMMARY

It's the moon's "billionth birthday." She's sullen because no one has ever given her what she really wants; a beautiful flannel nightgown with stars all over it, like the one she sees on Ellen's clothesline. The moon goes into town to look for one just like it, finds the gown in a store, and happily puts it on. Dressed in her gown, however, the moon is invisible, and all the living things on earth miss her a lot. The sun convinces the moon to take off the gown, and reluctantly she does so. But some nights still she tries it on again, goes to sleep, and dreams she is sleeping in a feather bed with Ellen.

READING STRATEGIES

PRE-READING

As children discuss their own observations of the moon and how it seems to change its shape and sometimes disappear entirely, ask if they ever imagine a "face" in the moon. Does it look happy? sad? angry? Introduce the word *sullen* as you show the book cover and read the title. Ask children to keep a careful eye on the moon's face as you read the book to find some hints about the meaning of *sullen.*

WHILE READING

Invite children to elaborate on the story by telling what the moon is doing and feeling in the pictures that go with each page. Call attention to the new expression on the moon's face as she leaves the store in her nightgown and joyfully sails out of town. Explain that now the moon isn't sullen anymore, and encourage children to tell what *sullen* must mean (to pout, be a little angry, gloomy, in bad humor, cross, cranky). To add to children's vocabulary, encourage them to tell from the pictures how the people and animals on earth feel when they can't see the moon anymore. What words describe the moon's feelings? Invite volunteers to tell why they would miss the moon if it disappeared forever, and how they know from their real-life observations that this won't happen.

BUILDING THE SCIENCE CONNECTION

Review the book illustration that shows part of the globe (earth) and the moon in her nightgown high above it. Invite students to compare the picture with the globe. Challenge them to find the corresponding areas on the globe. Point out the United States on the globe and affix a colored sticker to your area.

Ask a volunteer to be the moon by holding the table tennis ball outstretched toward the globe and moving very slowly all around it. As the child is moving, explain that he or she is showing the orbit, or circular path, that the real moon follows through the sky. Explain that it takes the real moon about 28 days to orbit all around the earth to the place where it started.

Engage the class in a "Moon Call" like the ones shown in the dialogue balloons in the story illustrations. As the table tennis ball moon moves over the sticker, the children call "Welcome back, moon!" When the moon has reached the opposite side of the globe, the children call "Come back, Moon!" Continue the simulation with other volunteers. During the enactment, you or your students may wish to add your own dialogue, improvising on the story and using the word "orbit" to describe the moon's motion.

Conclude the activity by asking children what they would say to Ellen, the girl in the story, to help her understand that she will see the moon in the sky again, even though she may not see it tonight.

EXTENDING THE SCIENCE CONNECTION

Activity. To help children extend the concept of an orbit and understand the relative positions in space of the sun, earth, and moon, invite three volunteers to play the parts of the sun (the kickball), earth (the tennis ball), and earth's moon (the table tennis ball). Explain that these balls don't represent the actual scale of the sun, earth, and moon. The scale would be: a grain of sand for the moon; a pea for earth; a large beach ball for the sun.

In this simulation, the sun stands still in the center of a large demonstration area. Ask "earth" to move very slowly in a very large orbit around "sun," while "moon" moves more quickly in its orbit around "earth." Discuss how both earth and moon have orbits. Point out the difference in what they are orbiting around. (Earth orbits the sun; the moon orbits the earth and the sun.)

Conclude the activity by asking participants to find the meaning of the word *satellite* to figure out how the word refers to both earth and the moon. As a prompt from the story, you might use the following: Ellen says, "I understand now that the moon orbits around earth. But earth just stays in the same ol' place, doesn't it?"

Further Reading. K–1 reading partners might enjoy reading together Satoshi Kitamura's *UFO*. They can then draw pictures of what the space traveler sees as he nears earth and its moon. Children reading on a higher level can enjoy James Thurber's *Many Moons* and then discuss how the princess is both right and wrong about the moon!

FOLLOW-UP ACTIVITIES
ORAL LANGUAGE/ART/DRAMA: MOON SKITS

Children can work in groups to design nightgowns for the Sullen Moon. They can then improvise plays in which the moon is orbiting earth, trying on her various gowns, and getting reactions from people and animals below her. Suggest that members work together to make a variety of gowns.

Specific group roles can be assigned: two or three playwrights to organize the group's ideas into a general plot for the skit, actors to play the part of the moon and the other characters, a coach or director to suggest when each actor should speak and perform, and a narrator/emcee to introduce the play to the class and tell what is happening.

Encourage the classroom audience to listen so that they can tell what they like best about each skit.

WRITING: BILLIONTH-BIRTHDAY PRESENTS

At the center of a bulletin board, put a large picture of the moon. Add a head that reads, "What Shall We Give the Moon for Her Billionth Birthday?" Suggest to children that now that the moon has all the nightgowns she can possibly use, other gifts might be in order.

Briefly discuss other possible gifts emanating from the story or from the science investigation. For example, a feather bed, a clothesline or an electric washer and dryer for the gowns, a poem or sentence from humans or other animals about why they like the moon, a statement of a fact about the moon's orbit, a picture of a happy Ellen enjoying the moonlight, a list of words that mean "moon" in different languages (refer to the same book illustration as in Building the Science Connection).

Then invite each child to make a labelled picture of the gift he or she will give the moon on her birthday. Attach children's drawings to the bulletin board display with yarn or strips of colored construction paper. Invite gift-givers to tell the class about their presents and why the moon will not be sullen anymore when she gets them.

SOCIAL STUDIES: MAPS FOR THE MOON

Ask children to imagine that the Sullen Moon is coming to their community to look for a nightgown. She needs a map to guide her through the neighborhood. Review the illustrations in the book that show a bird's-eye (moon's-eye!) view of Ellen's town. Ask your students to make picture maps of their area for the Sullen Moon, leading her to a store where she can get a nightgown. Encourage your mapmakers to label or otherwise identify streets and other place names. As children show their finished maps, invite them to tell stories about the moon's quest, tracing her routes on the maps.

MATH: MOON MILES

Invite interested students to find out how far the moon is from earth (about 238,857 miles). Then, to help children get a concept of what one mile is, display and discuss a local map with a mileage scale on it. Point out areas that are within one mile of your school. Ask children if they ever walked that far. If possible, organize a class outing in which your students walk that

From *Science & Stories*, Grades K–3, published by GoodYearBooks. Copyright © 1994 Hilarie N. Staton and Tara McCarthy.

distance. Afterwards discuss what a mile feels like when one is walking. How long does it take to walk a mile? Discuss what is meant by a car that can go "100 miles an hour," or a plane that can go "500 miles an hour."

APPLYING THE SCIENCE CONCEPT:

✓ Distribute Activity Sheet 12. Explain that the picture shows Earth and the moon. Ask children to color the moon yellow and the earth green and blue. Discuss the words at the bottom of the sheet. Give children the option of either copying the labels where they belong on the diagram, or cutting them out and pasting them in the correct spot. Ask children to draw either a sullen or happy face on the moon. As children show their finished pictures, invite them to tell why the moon is feeling sullen or happy.

The Nightgown of the Sullen Moon

Name _____   Date _____

MOON TRIP

DIRECTIONS
Follow the directions your teacher gives you.

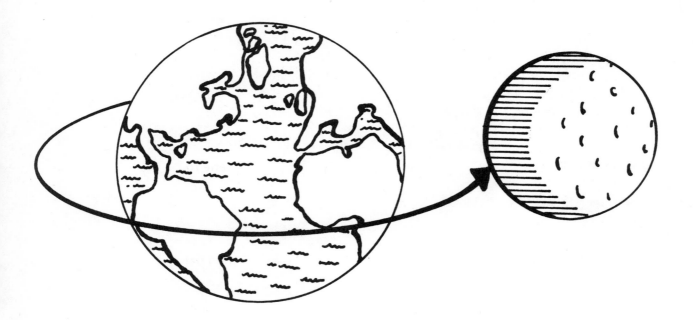

Earth   **Moon**   **Orbit**

From *Science & Stories*, Grades K-3, published by GoodYearBooks. Copyright © 1994 Hilarie N. Staton and Tara McCarthy.

LESSON 13

LITERATURE:
Katy and the Big Snow
Virginia Lee Burton (Houghton Mifflin, 1971)

SCIENCE:
Energy and Matter

UNDERSTANDING:
Energy can be transferred by changing the positions of objects.

INQUIRY SKILLS:
Observing, recording data, identifying variables, generalizing, decision-making

AHEAD *of* TIME

WHAT YOU'LL NEED

For Building the Science Connection
- several shoe boxes with string loops attached to one end
- objects of various weights to place in the shoe boxes, such as polystyrene foam, popcorn, rocks, marbles, cloth, empty and full cans
- small spring scales

For Follow-Up Activities
- make arrangements for a field trip or class speaker (Writing)
- art materials for writing thank-you notes and illustrations—construction paper, crayons, colored pencils, or markers (Writing)
- art materials for making a model of Geoppolis—empty cereal boxes, large sheets of brown paper, construction paper, straws and spools for street lamps, small empty boxes turned inside out for cars and other vehicles, crayons or markers for drawings, scissors, glue (Geography)
- art materials for making a sculpture of a machine—empty cereal and other boxes turned inside out, dowels, parts of broken toys (Art/Sculpture)
- crayons, colored pencils, or markers for coloring Activity Sheet 13 (Applying the Science Concept)

STORY SUMMARY

Katy was a big, strong, heavy-duty red crawler tractor. She was used for jobs by the Highway Department of Geoppolis. In the summer, Katy worked on building roads and once pulled a steamroller out of the pond. However, in the winter, she didn't come out until there was a BIG snow. One year, the snow was so deep the snowplows broke down. The roads were blocked and the city came to a standstill—

except for Katy. Slowly and steadily, Katy plowed out the police, the postmaster, and the railway station, as well as the telephone and electric company. She plowed out people with emergencies and people whose job it was to help them, such as the water department, hospitals, the fire department, and the airport. Only when all of Geoppolis had been plowed did Katy go home and rest.

READING STRATEGIES

PRE-READING

If students are unfamiliar with snow or snow storms, use videos, pictures, and newspaper articles to introduce them. You can make snowballs by having students mold crushed ice into balls. You may also want to review the seasons.

Using the picture on the first page of the story, introduce a crawler tractor and what it does. Invite students to identify Katy's various features. With more advanced students, discuss horsepower. Then turn to pages 4 and 5 and invite students to name, describe, and compare the equipment pictured. You may want to share some brochures from heavy equipment companies. Encourage students to identify similarities and differences between these machines.

WHILE READING

Read the story to students. Stop at various points and ask students to describe the type of work being done. Encourage them to identify the changes occurring.

BUILDING THE SCIENCE CONNECTION

Encourage students to name all the types of work Katy could do. Explain that in science, *work* means pushing or pulling an object to cause motion. Ask students to think of different types of work, from writing (pushing a pencil) to moving dirt. Invite students to bring in newspaper and magazine pictures that show someone or something doing work. Have stu-

dents categorize the pictures under headings such as "Easy Work," "Medium Work," and "Hard Work." Build a collage with students' pictures arranged to show the easiest work at one end and the hardest at the other, with the medium work arranged between.

Have students form small groups, or do this investigation as a class demonstration. Fill three or more shoe boxes with objects of different weights. Leave one shoe box empty. Have students examine the boxes and predict which will be the easiest and hardest to move.

Review the scientific definition of work. (See above.) Explain that in order to move something, "force" must be used. Force is the amount of push or pull necessary to get the object moving. When force is used to move something, the result is work.

During this activity have students determine how much force it takes to move each box. Attach a spring scale, with the scale side up, to the loop at the end of the empty shoe box. Place it on a slick surface, such as a plastic garbage bag. Have one student insert a finger in the end of the scale and pull gently and steadily. When it is moving slowly and smoothly, another student reads the scale. This is the amount of force necessary to move that shoe box. A third student can act as recorder and record the force on a chart like the one on the following page.

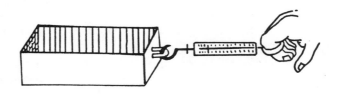

Students should switch jobs and repeat the procedure with at least two more boxes, each filled with different objects. Students then identify the box that took the least force and the one that took the most force.

From *Science & Stories*, Grades K-3, published by GoodYearBooks. Copyright © 1994 Hilarie N. Staton and Tara McCarthy.

	Box's contents	Force necessary to move
Box 1		
Box 2		
Box 3		

Invite the groups to share their findings with the class. Guide the discussion, so that students form the generalization that it takes more force to move heavier objects. Suggest they apply that generalization to the story in order to answer the question, "Why could Katy do the jobs that the snow plows couldn't?" (The snow was so heavy that the less powerful snow plows couldn't do the work. Katy had more energy so she could.)

EXTENDING THE SCIENCE CONNECTION

Interested second- or third-grade students can apply concepts relating to simple machines to the shoe box activity. They can investigate which simple machines can make moving the heavy boxes easier. They can measure the force it takes to move a heavy box by just pulling, pushing, lifting, or using a ramp (inclined plane) or wheels (round pencils). Encourage students to record their results and share them with the class.

Further Reading. *Katy and the Big Snow* can also be used to teach weather or seasonal concepts. For instance, it could be used as one of a series of books on snow, winter, or weather and its effects on humans. This unit might include other books, such as Jane Yolen's *Owl Moon* or David Wiesner's *Hurricane.*

FOLLOW-UP ACTIVITIES
ORAL LANGUAGE: EVERYONE WORKS

Review the scientific definition of work and then have students compare its meaning to work as used in the following sentence: Jose's father works as a doctor. Help them identify the other definition of work as "having to do with an occupation or employment." Ask students to list all the jobs, or work, people do. If the list is short, have students interview people about their jobs. Include the jobs discussed in *Katy and the Big Snow.* Have students form cooperative learning groups. Invite each group to investigate and illustrate one job done by people in *Katy and the Big Snow.* The group can practice reading the section of the book dealing with that job and perform a choral reading as you reread the book. Invite students to share what the people with that job do to help the town and the type of work, according to the scientific definition, these people do. (For example, the postal worker expends energy to move mail from the bag into the mailbox. Ambulance workers move injured people.)

WRITING: HEAVY EQUIPMENT SAVES THE DAY

Activity 1. Take a field trip to a local highway department garage or invite someone from the highway department to speak to the class about the equipment the department uses. Ask that they use pictures, charts, and, if possible, allow

a close examination of the equipment. Invite the students to write thank-you notes and create illustrations to send to the department or speaker.

Activity 2. After students are familiar with heavy equipment, write a class story about one piece of machinery, using *Katy and the Big Snow* as a model. Invite the class to brainstorm about the equipment they know and emergencies that could happen and then choose an item from each list to plan the action. Volunteers can suggest plot ideas and list their ideas randomly on the chalkboard. Encourage students to choose several ideas, organize them, and dictate sentences about them. Write the sentences exactly as they are said. After the story is complete, or the next day, edit the story with the class. Encourage students to evaluate it and to suggest changes, additions, or deletions to the story's organization, sentence sequence, descriptions, sentence structure, grammar, or spelling. You might want to stress the concepts you are teaching in other parts of the curriculum. You, or individual students, can create a final, edited copy of the story to display or add to a book of class stories.

GEOGRAPHY: A MODEL OF GEOPPOLIS
Invite students to make a three-dimensional model of Geoppolis by making each building mentioned or shown in the book. Here's an easy, quick way to make buildings from cereal boxes. Carefully unglue the boxes and turn them inside out to get clean gray or white surfaces for coloring. Draw building features on the boxes before regluing. Create a large model of the town by placing these buildings on large sheets of brown paper that show the streets. Discuss map stars and directions (north, south, east, west, and the intermediary directions like northwest if appropriate to the students' ability). Place a direction star on the map.

Using toy cars or people, invite students to take a tour of their Geoppolis map. Act out the story with one student moving Katy, and others playing the various roles described in the story. Finally, a direction game can be played. You or students give specific directions, such as "Go west two blocks," to get around town.

HEALTH: TUNE-UP FOR YOUR BODY
Encourage students to draw parallels between Katy being kept in top condition by her mechanic and kids caring for their own health. They can create a class chart of all the ways they "take care" of themselves, from brushing teeth and eating right to check-ups by a doctor. Create analogies with students that compare mechanical devices and people. An example is: Katy is to a mechanic's tune-up as John is to a doctor's check-up.

ART/SCULPTURE: MACHINE ART
Invite students to build a sculpture of a machine, either a real one like Katy or an imaginary one. Suggest they use a variety of materials, such as cardboard boxes, clay, found objects, dowels and old broken toys. Allow students to share their sculptures and describe the type of work their machines do.

✓ APPLYING THE SCIENCE CONCEPT:
Distribute Activity Sheet 13 to students. Discuss the work (in the scientific sense) that is being done in each picture. Have students circle the picture in each pair that shows the most force. Then have them color the one picture on the whole page that shows more force than any other.

From *Science & Stories, Grades K–3,* published by GoodYearBooks. Copyright © 1994 Hilarie N. Staton and Tara McCarthy.

Katy and the Big Snow

Name _____ Date _____

PEOPLE AND WORK

DIRECTIONS

Look at each pair of pictures. For each pair, circle the one picture that shows the most force. Color the one picture on the page that shows more force than any other picture.

LESSON 14

LITERATURE:
The Magic Fan
Keith Baker (Harcourt Brace Jovanovich, 1989)

SCIENCE:
Energy and Matter

UNDERSTANDING:
Matter and energy interact to make changes.

INQUIRY SKILLS:
Observing, recording data, creating models, predicting, identifying variables

AHEAD *of* TIME

WHAT YOU'LL NEED

For Building the Science Connection
- small plastic toy boats both with and without sails
- deep, flat baking pan filled with water
- deep container
- two bricks
- small diameter stick

For Follow-Up Activities
- art materials for drawing sequential pictures—construction paper, crayons, colored pencils, or markers (Oral Language)
- newspaper articles, magazine pictures, or video clips covering recent natural disasters (Writing)
- art materials for making math cards—ruler, crayons or colored pencils, large index cards (Math)
- art materials for making fans and kites—light crêpe paper, tissue paper, straws or light sticks, string for kites, construction paper, old manila file folders for fans, watercolors, markers, crayons, scissors, glue (Art/Math)

STORY SUMMARY
Yoshi loved to build, but ran out of ideas until he found a magic fan. Each time the fan showed him something (a boat, a kite, and a bridge) he built it, although the village people could not understand why. Then when a tsunami came, the village people rushed onto his bridge and watched the water destroy the village. Although he lost his fan, Yoshi had plenty to build. He knew he'd help rebuild the town, and then he'd build wonderful and unusual devices from his own ideas. He finally realized that all along the ideas had been his own, not the fan's.

READING STRATEGIES

PRE-READING
Display a fan for students. Invite them to list all the ways it could be used. Encourage them to use their imaginations to suggest what a magic fan might do.

Remind students that the names we have for some things come from other languages. After inviting their suggestions, give examples familiar to students, such as taco, pizza, and kindergarten. Write the word *tsunami* on the chalk-

From *Science & Stories*, Grades K–3, published by GoodYearBooks. Copyright © 1994 Hilarie N. Staton and Tara McCarthy.

board and pronounce it (tzŏŏ nä mē). Explain that *tsunami* is a Japanese word for a huge wave of water caused by the movement of the earth under the ocean. After you locate Japan on a map and identify it as a place that has tsunamis, explain that there is a tsunami in the story. Have students predict what they think will happen to the village when the tsunami comes.

WHILE READING

Read the book *The Magic Fan* to students. Ask them to suggest answers to Yoshi's questions (on the left-hand pages) before you turn the fan or read the right-hand pages. Encourage unusual, creative, and "magical" answers.

BUILDING THE SCIENCE CONNECTION

To introduce the concept that matter interacts with different energy sources in different ways, ask students to recall the effects water and air had on Yoshi's creations. Reread the final page of the book and have students predict what effect water and air might have on each of the things Yoshi plans to build.

Small groups or the whole class can watch and participate in the following demonstrations. After each demonstration, have students write or draw a journal entry that includes a sketch or diagram and a written summary of what they observed.

Demonstration 1. Fill a deep, flat baking pan with water. When the water is calm, place two toy boats, one with a sail and one without, carefully on the water. When the water is calm again, have students blow gently on the water, not on the boats. Have them repeat this blowing more forcefully. Encourage students to share their journal entries about what happened to each boat.

Demonstration 2. Use the same setup as for Demonstration 1, but have students blow on the sail and above the non-sailboat, with gentle and then forceful breaths. Encourage students to write another journal entry and to share those entries with another student.

Demonstration 3. Place a brick on the bottom of a deeper container. Place a second brick so that one end rests on the first brick and the other on the bottom of the container, as shown here:

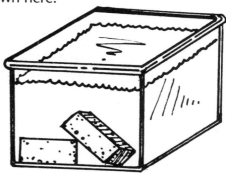

Fill the container with water so that there is at least two inches of water above the bricks. Place the boats on the surface of the water. Use a small stick to gently push the upper brick off the flat one. The resulting wave is similar to a tsunami. Have students observe and record what happened.

After students have recorded all three demonstrations, invite volunteers to share their journal entries. Encourage students to identify the similarities and differences in each demonstration. You might want to cover understandings such as height of waves, source and strength of motion (energy), and how motion affects people (helps sailboats travel, makes people seasick, or destroys people's property).

EXTENDING THE SCIENCE CONNECTION

Further Reading. Second- or third-grade students can use the book *The Boy Who Held Back the Sea* by Thomas Locker, or other retellings of the boy with his finger in the dike, to study ways people control water. David Wiesner's book *Hurricane* also discusses the power of wind and rain.

FOLLOW-UP ACTIVITIES

ORAL LANGUAGE: BEACH DAYS

Invite students to describe experiences they've had at the beach. Suggest they include information about how the air, sun, waves, and sand looked, smelled, and felt, as well as what changes each caused (water destroying a sand castle, wind blowing off a hat). Interested students may want to illustrate their experiences. For those who have had no such experiences, read a book, such as Ken Robbins' *Beach Days* or Gene Zion's *Harry by the Sea,* from which students can create an imaginary visit.

ORAL LANGUAGE/SCIENCE: NATURAL CHANGES

Form several small groups. Have each group choose and discuss one form of natural energy that causes motion (wind, waves, earth movement). In a brainstorming session, each group lists objects that their force could move and what would happen when the objects were moved. After students have created the list, they can choose one object and imagine a situation where the force moves that object. They might draw a set of sequential pictures with accompanying text to show what happens to the object. One group might do a set of pictures like the following:

From *Science & Stories*, Grades K–3, published by GoodYearBooks. Copyright © 1994 Hilarie N. Staton and Tara McCarthy.

Each group member is responsible for one picture and sentence in the sequence. If you have students who have trouble with art or writing, allow them to trade jobs so one does more art and the other more writing. Invite each group to present its sequence to the class. The class can put scrambled sets of pictures into the correct order to practice sequencing skills. Or they can describe the proper sequence of pictures using appropriate key words, such as first and second.

WRITING: DEAR FRIEND

Reread *The Magic Fan* to students. Discuss the destruction caused by the tsunami. If there has been a recent natural disaster, share newspaper articles, magazine pictures, and TV news clips of it. Invite students to suggest ways they could help the victims. Suggest that each student write a letter to a child in Yoshi's village or to a victim of a real disaster. Remind students that their purpose is to communicate their feelings to the person. Have students write first drafts and then work with a peer editor to check for spelling and effective communication. Have students make clean copies of their letters to send to real people or to Keith Baker, the author/illustrator of *The Magic Fan*.

MATH: HOW FAR

Third graders might make a class set of math word problem cards. Each card should show a picture of something that has moved and be accompanied by a question about the distance it moved. To answer the question, students must measure the distance the object moved. For instance, the picture might be of a ship, with two spots marked on the ocean. The question might be as follows: A ship traveled from point A to point B. If 1 inch equals 50 miles, how far did it travel? After the problems have been written on scratch paper, have students find partners to solve the problems and make editing suggestions. The problems can then be recopied onto 4" x 6" index cards to be used in a math center or as later math assignments.

LITERATURE: WINDY POEMS

Introduce students to poems about wind, the moon, and the sea. Read a few poems, such as those in Ann Jones' *Reflections*, Caroline Bauer's *Windy Day: Stories and Poems*, or Lisa Peters' *The Sun, the Wind, and the Rain*, to students. Then have partners choose several poems to read aloud to each other with varying tones and phrasing. Have them perfect the choral reading of one poem and perform it for the class.

ART/MATH: MAGIC FANS AND GLORIOUS KITES

Fans (with magic pictures on them) and kites (which could see the world) are natural art activities to do after reading *The Magic Fan*. Make fans as part of a math lesson on measuring or dividing spaces into equal parts.

Activity 1. Have students draw a simple or complex scene that might appear on a "magic fan." Then they measure and mark the page into equal sections and fold it along those lines. Use accordion folds. Secure the base with a staple or paper clip. Fans can then be opened, admired, and shared with others.

Activity 2. More advanced students might enjoy making kites, such as those described in L. Somerville's *How to Make a Kite*. They can design simple or elaborate creations that represent various animals or characters in folk and fairy tales from various cultures.

SOCIAL STUDIES: LIFE IN OLD JAPAN

Thumb through *The Magic Fan* with students. Invite them to find examples of life in old Japan. Begin a class chart, similar to the one below, on which students can record their findings. They can add information by placing pictures,

sentences, and phrases in the appropriate categories.

Have individuals, partners, or small groups read one or more of the following books about life in old Japan: Masako Matsuno's *A Pair of Red Clogs*, Momokoto Ishii's *The Tongue-Cut Sparrow*, or Patricia Montgomery Newton's *The Five Sparrows: A Japanese Folktale.* Be sure the stories take place in historic Japan, so that students do not confuse life in the past with life in Japan today. Have students add details from their reading to various categories on the chart or to new categories. Divide the class into groups. Invite each group to write a paragraph and make a dramatic presentation that reflects the information under one category on the chart. The paragraphs can be combined and edited to create a class essay on the culture of old Japan.

APPLYING THE SCIENCE CONCEPT:

☑ Hand out Activity Sheet 14 to students. Discuss each picture and the two forces given (water and air). Have students match each object to the type of energy necessary to make it move. After they are done, invite volunteers to share the visual clues that helped them to decide on their answers.

From *Science & Stories*, Grades K-3, published by GoodYearBooks. Copyright © 1994 Hilarie N. Staton and Tara McCarthy.

The Magic Fan

Name _____ Date _____

ENERGY

DIRECTIONS

Draw a line from each picture to the type of energy that moves it.

Energy Source

Water

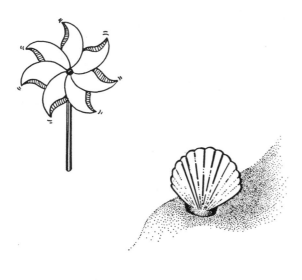

Air

LITERATURE:
How to Dig a Hole to the Other Side Of the World
Faith McNulty (Harper Trophy, 1979)

SCIENCE:
Energy and Matter

UNDERSTANDING:
Objects have distinct properties.

INQUIRY SKILLS:
Observing, classifying, inferring, creating models

AHEAD of TIME

WHAT YOU'LL NEED

For Building the Science Connection
- cutaway map of the inner Earth on large paper
- variety of rocks for each group
- box of soil containing a variety of components, screens, and a magnifying glass for each group
- globe (also used for Writing)

hot layers, and a jet-propelled submarine with a super cooling system, fireproof skin, and a drill on its nose. The explorer encounters different things on each level, such as diamonds, coal, bones, basalt, magma, water, and oil. As the heat gets more intense, the explorer goes through steam, magma, the hot mantle, and the even hotter cores of melted iron and rock. Finally the explorer arrives at the center of the earth with its lack of gravity and the meeting of all directions. The submarine comes out in the Indian Ocean and travels home by sail.

STORY SUMMARY

This book tells what you'd see if you traveled through the center of the Earth. The child explorer digs a hole through every level: topsoil, granite crust, basalt layer, the Earth's mantle, the inner core, the outer core, and back out into the Indian Ocean. The explorer encounters problems and suggests solutions. For instance, a friend is needed to pull buckets of clay or gravel out of the hole. The explorer uses different technology on different levels: a drilling machine to get through the crust, a diving suit for pools of water, an asbestos diving suit to keep cool in

READING STRATEGIES

PRE-READING

Ask students if the ground is the same everywhere you dig. Invite them to share different things they might find in the ground and specific examples, such as rocks in the park and sand at the beach. Guide the discussion to the conclusion that there are many different types of rocks, soil, and other landforms. Brainstorm all the things students think they would find if they were to dig a hole straight through the earth. Write this list on the chalkboard, so students can review it after reading the book.

Review with students what happens when you heat something, such as water. (Heating solids can form liquids or gases. Heating liquids forms gases.) Discuss the three states of matter and ask students to predict whether rocks can change into liquids with enough heat.

With students, compare the reading strategies useful for reading a story for enjoyment and those useful for reading a book filled with facts and details. Suggest students make summaries to recall the facts after they read each page.

WHILE READING

Read the book, but stop after each page and help students summarize the important concepts, vocabulary, and facts that were on that page. Model a summary of at least the first page by describing how you make decisions about what to include. Your dialogue might go something like this: "Let's see. A summary has to include the most important ideas and words on this page. What was on the page? I know, it told about starting to dig in the soft top layer called loam which is dirt, dead worms, and rocks. The next layer down is clay, gravel, or sand. I'd need a friend to pull out the buckets of dirt from the hole. I think that's all that was important on the page."

If students are already familiar with the concepts presented in the book, do the summaries by layers rather than by pages. If students need extra reinforcement to learn the vocabulary, review the meaning of each new term as the word occurs. You can also create a class chart of important terms as you read.

SCIENCE STRATEGIES
BUILDING THE SCIENCE CONNECTION
Activity 1. When you have finished the book, invite students to go back to their chart of what they thought they'd find inside the Earth. Add items they did not include. Invite volunteers to share why or why not they think the events could ever happen. Encourage them to share why they'd like to make this trip or why they'd never want to make the trip.

Activity 2. Reread the book with students to find the information necessary to label a cutaway map of the inner Earth. Label each layer with its correct label and discuss what is found in each. Encourage students to identify the properties of what is found in each layer and exactly what the explorer saw.

Activity 3. Hold up two objects, such as chalk and a book. Invite students to list everything they can observe about each object. Be sure students include what the objects look like, how they feel, how they smell, how they sound when dropped, what they're made of, how hard they are, their size, and their weight. After students generate a list, create several categories of characteristics, such as size, shape, color, height, mass.

With the class, create a chart for examining rock characteristics, which might look like the chart below.

Have students form groups. Give each group four to five rocks to examine carefully. Have them record their findings on a copy of the class chart. Suggest that students categorize the rocks by some specific criteria, such as size (big

	Rock 1	Rock 2	Rock 3	Rock 4
Weight				
Hardness				
Size and Shape				
Looks Like				
Uniform or Composite				

rocks, small rocks), composition (uniform rocks, composite rocks), or color (blue rocks, red rocks). Students should then sequence their rocks within that criteria (largest to smallest, softest to hardest, darkest to lightest). Invite students to share their classifications, sequences, and criteria.

EXTENDING THE SCIENCE CONNECTION

Activity 1. Suggest that more able or interested students research a specific type of matter and the conditions it needs to change state (i.e., liquid into gas). Using their research, students can draw a chart to illustrate the temperature and conditions necessary to change states. They can present their findings to the class and compare and contrast their findings with findings on other types of matter.

Activity 2. Third-grade or more able students can form groups to investigate how different types of rocks are formed. After groups of three are formed, each student in the group chooses a different type of rock (igneous, metamorphic, or sedimentary). Students from different groups studying the same types of rock should meet in "expert" groups. They research that specific type of rock, decide on important information, and create visuals to share with their groups. Then the experts return to their original groups and teach the other two group members about the type of rock they studied. For evaluation, groups or individuals can classify rocks, using the criteria taught to them by their team members.

Further Reading. Second- and third-grade students might enjoy reading Joanna Cole's book *The Magic School Bus Inside the Earth*. This not only contains related information, but has suggestions for individual reports and projects.

FOLLOW-UP ACTIVITIES

ORAL LANGUAGE: NOT JUST DIRT

Have students form groups of three to four students. Each student in the group can have a different job, such as recorder, examiner, sorter, praiser, or runner. Each group examines a box of mixed soil. Suggest that they use screens and a magnifying glass to identify various components. Encourage each group to create an oral and visual presentation that includes an oral part for each group member and a chart or illustrations.

WRITING: EARTH SENTENCES

Create a vocabulary list from the book or use the one created during the reading of the book. Suggest students write several sentences using at least two words from the list in each sentence. Have students share their sentences with partners, who check for both meaning and writing errors.

WRITING: INTERVIEWING THE INNER-EARTH EXPLORER

Examine and discuss question-and-answer interviews with the class. Develop a sequence of how an interviewer might do an interview. (Research a topic, write questions, ask questions, write the answers, organize, and then write the article). Invite pairs of students to write at least four questions they'd like to ask the book's explorer. Suggest that their questions use their new vocabulary and knowledge about the earth. Interviewers can also ask about the feelings the explorer had during his trip. Have one pair of students ask another pair their questions. The second pair answers the questions as if they were the explorer. Pairs can then switch roles. Each pair organizes and edits its questions and answers into a magazine article. If your class has desktop publishing capability, students can lay out, illustrate, and publish their magazine articles.

From *Science & Stories, Grades K–3,* published by GoodYearBooks. Copyright © 1994 Hilarie N. Staton and Tara McCarthy.

From *Science & Stories*, Grades K-3, published by GoodYearBooks. Copyright © 1994 Hilarie N. Staton and Tara McCarthy.

GEOGRAPHY: WHERE IN THE WORLD ARE WE?

The goal of this game is to familiarize students with the globe and with place names around the world. Point out, on a globe, where the explorer came out (Indian Ocean) and where he must have started if the hole was straight. Then have students form two teams (four if you have enough globes). One team names any spot on the globe where an explorer will start a hole. The other team confers to determine where that explorer will come out after digging a straight hole through the earth. If correct, the team gets a point and the teams switch roles. If incorrect, the team does not get a point, but roles are still switched. Make the game easier or harder by giving visual clues, more or less information about a place, or time limits for team conferences.

APPLYING THE SCIENCE CONCEPT:

☑ Distribute Activity Sheet 15 to students. Explain that Peter and Jackie have found all the things pictured in their soil sample. Name each item for students. Have students sort at least four of the items into a classification of their choice. They should label a blank page with the name of their classification and paste all the pictures that fit that class on the page. Then they should list all the common characteristics of the items they've included in that classification. You might want to work one example with students; or you might give them sample classifications, such as big, small, manufactured, or from a tree.

How to Dig a Hole to the Other Side Of the World

Name _____ Date _____

SEE WHAT WE'VE FOUND

DIRECTIONS
These are the things Peter and Jackie found in their soil sample. Cut the pictures apart. Sort some pictures into a group that goes together. Tell why all of the member of that group belong together.

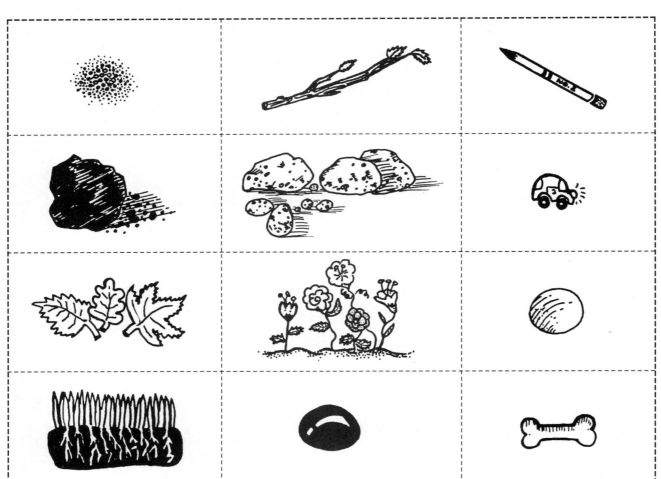

LESSON 16

LITERATURE:
Hill of Fire
Thomas P. Lewis (Harper & Row, 1971)

SCIENCE:
Patterns of Change

UNDERSTANDING:
Many materials change in volume when they are heated.

INQUIRY SKILLS:
Observing, predicting, inferring, manipulating materials, identifying variables

AHEAD *of* TIME

WHAT YOU'LL NEED

For Pre-Reading
- map of Mexico, detailed enough to show the Paricutín volcano

For Building the Science Connection
- store-bought standard pastry dough
- jam or jelly
- teaspoons
- plastic cup or round cookie cutter
- nail or a knitting needle
- rolling pin
- flour
- muffin tin
- conventional oven (not a microwave) (You'll be doing the actual baking.)

For Extending the Science Connection (for each group)
- a few hard-boiled eggs, shells intact
- table knife
- black felt-tipped pens
- small stickers
- world map from encyclopedia or science textbook showing the "Ring of Fire" around the Pacific Ocean

For Follow-Up Activities
- (optional) tape recorders or video equipment (Oral Language)
- sample travel brochures from a tourist agency (Writing)
- art materials for producing travel brochures—construction paper, crayons or colored pencils (Writing)
- dictionary and almanac (Social Studies)

STORY SUMMARY

Only twice in recorded history has the birth of a volcano been seen by human eyes. *Hill of Fire* is an account of one of those times: the eruption of the Paricutín volcano in Mexico on February 20, 1943. The story is told through the eyes of a farmer and his son, who find their plow stuck in a hole. The hole quickly grows larger and emits smoke and noise. The man and the boy alert the townspeople, who watch for days as the volcano cone grows, coughs out rock and lava, and obviously threatens the town. The townspeople evacuate their homes, and the town is soon buried under rocks and lava. Undaunted, the people build another village nearby, continue their farming, and find an additional source of income as the new volcano becomes a tourist attraction.

READING STRATEGIES

PRE-READING

On a detailed map of Mexico, point out the Paricutín volcano, which is in the state of Michoacán, just west of the city of Morelia. Explain that the story students will read is true. As you show the book cover, ask students to infer what the "hill of fire" is. Ask them to listen to the story to find out how the volcano started, what happened as it grew, and how it affected the people who lived near it.

WHILE READING

Pause as necessary in your reading to help students define terms that may be new to them. Explain that lava is the hot, melted rock flowing from a volcano. If you have Spanish-speaking students in your classroom, encourage them to tell the meanings of *amigo* (friend) and *fiesta* (party). *El Monstruo* is defined within the context of the story.

Conclude the reading by discussing how the farmer felt at the beginning of the story: he was bored because nothing ever happened. Ask students why the farmer has changed the way he feels by the end of the story.

SCIENCE STRATEGIES

BUILDING THE SCIENCE CONNECTION

Explain that students will make "volcano tarts" to find out how volcanos come to be. Invite students to help prepare the tarts. Preheat the oven to 425°.

Have students roll out prepared pastry dough with the floured rolling pin. Then have them cut the dough into round shapes, using the floured rim of a cup or a cookie cutter. Demonstrate how to put one pastry circle at the bottom of each cup in the muffin tin. Explain that the circle stands for a layer of rock that is very, very deep inside the earth.

Have students put a teaspoon of jelly or jam on top of each pastry circle. Explain that the jelly stands for magma. *Magma* is what we call hot melted rocks when they're still inside the earth. Ask students if they remember what these rocks are called when they burst out of the earth (lava).

Show students how to put another pastry circle on top of the jam and pinch the edges of the two circles together firmly. Explain that this top circle stands for the surface of earth—the part we walk around on.

Demonstrate how to put a very small hole in the center in the top of the tart, using the nail or knitting needle. Explain that the hole stands for a slight weakness in earth's surface. Invite students to retell the part of the story where the plow sinks into the soil and a hole appears.

Put the tarts in the oven to bake. Then discuss the kind of energy that the oven produces (heat energy). Ask students to predict what will happen as the heat goes to work on the volcano tarts. Ask, "Will the jelly get hot? What do you think the heat will cause the jelly to do? Why?" Accept all predictions and explanations. Some students will correctly predict that the heat will force the jelly up through the hole in the top.

From *Science & Stories, Grades K-3*, published by GoodYearBooks. Copyright © 1994 Hilarie N. Staton and Tara McCarthy.

When the tarts are done, the jelly/magma will indeed have burst through the hole. Now the jelly/lava is running over the surface of the tart! As students eat their volcano tarts, review what happened: As the air inside the tart heated, it forced the jelly up until it "erupted" through the hole. Invite students to compare their volcano tarts with the real volcano in the story.

EXTENDING THE SCIENCE CONNECTION
Use this activity to help students visualize the basic structure of the earth. Divide the class into groups. Using the table knife, carefully cut several hard-boiled eggs in half breadthwise, doing as little damage to the shells as possible.

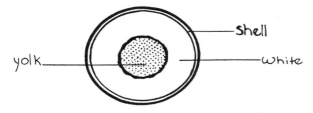

Ask students to examine the egg halves and explain what each part represents in the earth (the shell stands for the earth's surface, the white stands for the rocks beneath the surface, and the yolk stands for the earth's core, which is made of magma).

Explain that magma can rise up through cracks or passageways in rock. Ask students to use their felt-tipped pens to draw a line from the core (the yolk), through the rocks (the white of the egg), to just below the shell. Then have students remove a very small section of the shell just where their pen line ends. Explain that this stands for a weak spot in earth's crust.

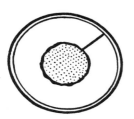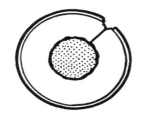

Ask students to imagine that the yellow core increases in heat and expands. From their reading of *Hill of Fire* and from their "volcano tart" activity, most students will be able to hypothesize what happens next: the magma erupts through earth's surface at the weak spot.

To conclude the activity, invite interested students to draw their own cross-sections of earth, using an encyclopedia as a reference source. Some students may enjoy doing research to find out where most observed volcanoes occur. Supply them with a world map and stickers so they can pinpoint the volcanoes, thereby discovering the "Ring of Fire"—the line around the rim of the Pacific Ocean where active volcanoes proliferate. Note: Paricutín, Mexico, is on the "Ring of Fire."

FOLLOW-UP ACTIVITIES
ORAL LANGUAGE: DRAMATIZING THE STORY
Invite groups of five or six students to dramatize *Hill of Fire* and present their plays to the class. Introduce the activity to the whole class by brainstorming to create a chalkboard list of major events in the story. Here is a sample list:

- The farmer complains about his boring days.
- The farmer and his son plow the field.
- The plow sinks into a hole.
- Smoke and noise come out of the hole.
- The farmer and his son run to the village and warn their neighbors.
- The townspeople watch and comment as the volcano grows.
- The townspeople flee, then build another village.
- Tourists come to see the volcano.
- The farmer says he is no longer bored.

Suggest that groups assign the acting roles (some group members can play more than one role), and appoint a director and a sound technician. The sound technician can improvise the booming, spitting, and rackety sounds of the volcano using found objects in the classroom or with tape-recorded effects. A group may also want to appoint a member as an announcer or narrator. Provide time for each group to practice its play at least once.

Arrange classroom time so that the groups can present their plays one after the other. If possible, videotape the plays and pan frequently to the audience to catch reactions. (Nothing is so encouraging to young actors as seeing their audience registering emotions of rapt attention, pleasure, or concern.) Show the tape and then discuss what was best about each play.

WRITING: A TRAVEL BROCHURE

Invite student partners to write and illustrate travel brochures about the Paricutín volcano. Suggest that their brochures give facts about the volcano that tell what, when, how, and where. The brochures can also state why tourists will enjoy seeing Paracutín, and include pictures of the volcano and the new town. If possible, have on hand several travel brochures (available free from any tourist agent) for students to peruse for ideas.

Encourage your writers to be imaginative as they make up a list of places to stay and other tourist tips usually included on travel brochures. After partners have shared their completed brochures with the class, put the brochures on a table in your reading or social studies center for students to read and discuss independently.

SOCIAL STUDIES: DISASTERS!

Capitalize on children's natural fascination with natural disasters by inviting student teams to find and write definitions of one of these: volcanic eruption, hurricane, blizzard, earthquake, tornado, flood, or tidal waves (tsunamis). Teams can then use almanacs to find out where these disasters have recently occurred and what their effects were on people, animals, and the envi-

ronment. Suggest that teams think of different ways to present their findings, such as charts, illustrated books, plays, murals, simulated TV news reports, or interviews with eyewitnesses.

Conclude the activity by discussing the concept of control. Why can't people control the disasters the students have investigated? Over what kinds of disasters do humans have some control? (air pollution, the decimation of species, the accumulation of garbage and waste, etc.). Loop back to the book by discussing how the townspeople recovered from a natural disaster by removing themselves to a new place and building a new town.

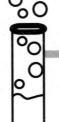

APPLYING THE SCIENCE CONCEPT:

✔ Distribute Activity Sheet 16. Discuss the picture and the labels, and clarify any terms students don't understand. Then explain that students are to write the labels on the lines where they belong on the cross-section of the volcano.

From *Science & Stories*, Grades K-3, published by GoodYearBooks. Copyright © 1994 Hilarie N. Staton and Tara McCarthy.

Hill of Fire

Name _____ Date _____

VOLCANO!

DIRECTIONS
Label the different parts
of a volcanic eruption
using the words below.

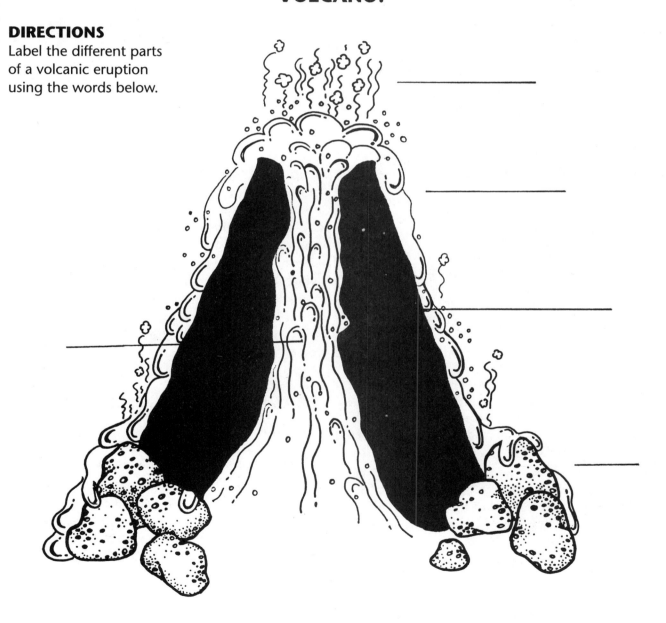

Labels: **volcano cone**   **magma**   **lava**   **hot rocks**   **steam**

LITERATURE:
Gregory, The Terrible Eater
Mitchell Sharmat (Scholastic, 1980)

SCIENCE:
Diversity

UNDERSTANDING:
Living things thrive when their needs are met.

INQUIRY SKILLS:
Classification, creating models, replicating, identifying variables

From *Science & Stories*, Grades K-3, published by GoodYearBooks. Copyright © 1994 Hilarie N. Staton and Tara McCarthy.

AHEAD *of* TIME

WHAT YOU'LL NEED

For Building the Science Connection
- pictures of various foods
- magazines, newspaper grocery store ads, etc., with pictures of foods
- large index cards

For Follow-Up Activities
- pictures or postcards of still lifes by famous artists (Art)
- scissors and tape or glue for Activity Sheet 17 (Applying the Science Concept)

STORY SUMMARY

Gregory is a young goat who is a terrible eater, for a goat. He likes fruits, vegetables, eggs, fish, bread, and butter instead of tin cans, boxes, rugs, or shirts. His parents are very upset by his eating habits. They keep trying to entice him into eating the foods they enjoy. They finally take him to Dr. Ram, who suggests they give Gregory one new food each day until he eats everything. So Gregory's parents add a shoelace to his spaghetti, a rubber heel to his string

beans, and serve the can with his vegetable soup. Soon Gregory likes everything and is eating objects from around the house between meals. His parents fear he will eat everything in the house, so they go to the town dump and get more "junk food" than Gregory can eat. Gregory eats until he gets a stomachache, which his parents tell him is from too much "junk." After a night of tossing and moaning, Gregory eats a "just right" breakfast: scrambled eggs, orange juice, and two pieces of waxed paper.

READING STRATEGIES

PRE-READING

Introduce the term *healthful diet* to students and have them identify what they think makes up a healthful diet for a person. Encourage them to suggest healthful diets for specific animals, such as their pets. Compare and contrast the diets of several different animals. Have students draw the conclusion that what is good for one animal might not be good for another.

Invite students to share what they know about goats, how they live, and what they eat. Keep a list of their suggestions. Encourage them

to identify the items that are facts and those that are fiction.

WHILE READING
Read the book to students. At appropriate points ask students what Gregory's parents think is wrong with the way Gregory is eating. Have them identify the reasons for the actions Gregory's parents take.

SCIENCE STRATEGIES
BUILDING THE SCIENCE CONNECTION
Make a large copy of the government's pyramid for good nutrition shown on page 88.

Discuss with students each of the components and evaluate a meal to see how it fits into the pyramid. Show students foods or pictures of food, such as an orange, a peanut butter sandwich, an ice cream cone, or a bowl of cereal. Demonstrate how someone might decide what part of the pyramid each food represents. For instance, if you show a bowl of corn flakes, you might say, "This is a bowl of corn flakes. Since corn is a grain, it belongs here. Since it is a small bowl, it would be only one serving. The milk in the cereal is from the dairy section of the pyramid. Since it is a small amount, it is half a serving. The banana on the cereal represents one serving from the fruit section." Encourage volunteers to show how they classify several simple items for the class.

Have students form small cooperative learning groups. Assign each member of the group a specific task such as runner (getting magazines and art materials), organizer (sorting the finished pictures), cutter, and checker (checking the facts). Invite groups to create sets of cards of various foods from each of the categories on the pyramid. They can cut out the pictures from magazines and grocery store ads, or draw their own pictures. Once the group has at least 10 cards, they make a chart like the one at the bottom of the page.

Each food card is placed under Food and its food group is identified. Invite each group to share its chart with the rest of the class. You might also want to create a class chart.

With the class, write specific questions to be answered about all the food categories. For example, one question may be, "How do these foods help us grow and keep healthy?" Use the same or new cooperative learning groups for this activity. Assign each member of the group a different food category. Have members from different groups who have the same food category work together. They become experts by investigating their category and answering the questions the class has written. They also gather pictures of foods that belong in their category. Students then return to their original groups to share their findings and make group pyramids with pictures from each member's specialty. Invite each group to write a daily menu which uses all the food groups. Have the groups share their pyramids and menus with the class. Compare the different menus to show different healthful diets.

Food	Breads	Fruit	Vegetables	Milk	Meat	Oil
beans						X
toast	X					
orange		X				

From *Science & Stories*, Grades K–3, published by GoodYearBooks. Copyright © 1994 Hilarie N. Staton and Tara McCarthy.

EXTENDING THE SCIENCE CONNECTION

Activity 1. Students can also explore where food originates. They can create a chart for common foods, such as hamburger, bread, or tuna. The chart should show the natural source of the food, where it goes (wheat goes to storage and then to a mill), how it is made into a specific form (a bakery makes flour into bread), and finally where it is sold to people. Students can share their charts. You can extend this activity by discussing how various communities throughout the world depend on each other for food.

Activity 2. Third-grade, interested, or more advanced students can investigate what constitutes a healthy diet for certain wild animals and how these animals are physically adapted to eat certain things. They might discuss a cow's stomachs or a lion's teeth. Suggest that students create visual and written profiles of their animals and their eating habits.

Further Reading. Invite second- and third-grade students to read *Cloudy with a Chance of Meatballs*. Encourage them to evaluate the diets of the people in the book to determine whether they had healthy diets when they depended on the weather for their food.

FOLLOW-UP ACTIVITIES

ORAL LANGUAGE: GREGORY'S STORY

After you have finished the book and discussed its events, have the students role-play their favorite scenes. Or assign groups different scenes to practice. Suggest the groups present their scenes in order. You might also play a sequencing game by presenting the scenes out of order and asking the class to put them into the correct sequence.

ORAL LANGUAGE: REMEMBER YOUR DIET

Invite students to perform a series of tasks using the food cards that they have made. Place the food cards along the chalkboard as if it were a cafeteria. Tell students, or have students tell each other, a list of foods to collect in a specific order. Use cue words (such as *first* and *second*) to help students. Demonstrate methods that you use to remember a list, such as grouping items by categories (if order is not required). You can also have students arrange a plate of foods, following your spoken directions. Use key words like *above, right, left,* and *next to*. Partners can give each other directions to create plates, meals, and menus.

ORAL LANGUAGE: A FUSSY EATER

Invite students to express their opinions about what made Gregory a terrible eater. Have them create a broad definition of a "terrible eater" and then apply it to a person. Invent a class portrait of a "fussy eater" by identifying what this person will and won't eat. Have small groups of students invent their own fussy eaters by drawing the people and surrounding them with things they like and don't like. Encourage the groups to plan silly meals that their fussy eaters might like, such as a dinner of spaghetti with chocolate sauce. Invite each group to share its fussy eater and silly meal with the class. Encourage students to share what is healthful and what is unhealthful about the fussy eaters' eating habits.

WRITING: BUSINESS LETTERS

Suggest that students write letters to a fast food company or to the makers of favorite foods, telling the companies what they like or don't like about their products and asking for the nutritional information about the products. Have student editors read the letters for clarity before final copies are made. Students can mail their final letters to the company. Encourage students to share the answers as they arrive.

SOCIAL STUDIES: CULTURAL FOOD

Have cooperative learning groups investigate the basic foods of different cultures. Encourage

From *Science & Stories*, Grades K-3, published by GoodYearBooks. Copyright © 1994 Hilarie N. Staton and Tara McCarthy.

each group to fit these foods into the government's pyramid and to draw a picture of a meal to share with the class. If you have a multicultural class, encourage students to investigate their own cultural food backgrounds and share the names of the foods with the class. If possible, with parental help, have an international nutritious food day. Invite parents to supply a variety of nutritious foods from various cultures.

ART: STILL LIFES
Display various still-life paintings by famous artists. Invite students to draw, paint, or make collages of still-life scenes. Suggest that each still life show more than one food group. Display the finished pictures for everyone to enjoy.

APPLYING THE SCIENCE CONCEPT:

☑ Distribute Activity Sheet 17 to students. Identify each picture. Tell students that they must use the pictured foods to help Peter and Jackie plan a healthful daily menu. To do this, students cut out the food pictures and organize them under the headings *breakfast, lunch,* and *dinner.* Remind students to consider the whole day's diet, not just fit everything into one meal. Encourage students to share their menus with the class.

Food Guide Pyramid
A Guide to Daily Food Choices

Use the Food Guide Pyramid to help you eat better every day — the Dietary Guidelines way! Start with plenty of Breads, Cereals, Rice, and Pasta; Vegetables; and Fruits. Add two to three servings from the Meat Group. Each of these food groups provides some, but not all, of the nutrients you need. No one food group is more important than another — for good health you need them all. Go easy on fats, oils, and sweets — the foods in the small tip of the Pyramid.

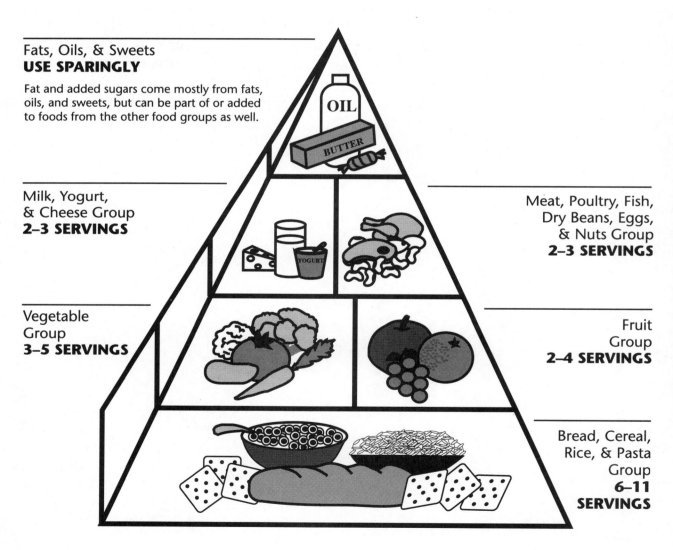

Fats, Oils, & Sweets
USE SPARINGLY

Fat and added sugars come mostly from fats, oils, and sweets, but can be part of or added to foods from the other food groups as well.

Milk, Yogurt, & Cheese Group
2–3 SERVINGS

Meat, Poultry, Fish, Dry Beans, Eggs, & Nuts Group
2–3 SERVINGS

Vegetable Group
3–5 SERVINGS

Fruit Group
2–4 SERVINGS

Bread, Cereal, Rice, & Pasta Group
6–11 SERVINGS

From *Science & Stories*, Grades K–3, published by GoodYearBooks. Copyright © 1994 Hilarie N. Staton and Tara McCarthy.

Gregory, the Terrible Eater

Name _____   Date _____

SATURDAY'S PLAN

DIRECTIONS

Help Peter and Jackie plan a healthful menu for Saturday. These are the foods they have around the house. Cut out the foods they will eat for each meal and paste them under the correct headings. Add some of your own food ideas too.

LESSON 18

LITERATURE:
Bringing the Rain to Kapiti Plain
Verna Aardema (Dial, 1981)

SCIENCE:
Scale and Structure

UNDERSTANDING:
Plants have parts that function to help the plant thrive.

INQUIRY SKILLS:
Observing, recording data, interpreting data, generalizing, manipulating materials

From *Science & Stories*, Grades K-3, published by GoodYearBooks. Copyright © 1994 Hilarie N. Staton and Tara McCarthy.

AHEAD of TIME

WHAT YOU'LL NEED

For Building the Science Connection
- two similar potted plants
- tray to set plants on
- aluminum foil or plastic wrap
- watering can

For Extending the Science Connection (for each group)
- carrot, complete with branch roots, stems, and leaves
- glass filled with water colored red with food dye
- vegetable knife

For Follow-Up Activities
- arrange for a class visit by a park ranger or other expert (Oral Language)
- art materials for making books—construction paper, colored pencils or crayons, scissors, glue, paper punch, yarn or brads for binding pages (Writing)
- encyclopedia or almanac (Math)
- art materials for drawing maps—paper, ruler, crayons or colored pencils (Geography)
- plants, seeds, soil, and containers for plant projects (Applying the Science Connection)

STORY SUMMARY

In this retelling of a tale from Kenya, a young herder, Ki-pat, watches his cattle go hungry and thirsty as a long drought afflicts Kapiti Plain. As the grass dies, the wild animals leave to find food and water elsewhere. Finally, to attempt to make the grass grow for his starving cattle, Ki-pat attaches a magic eagle feather to an arrow and shoots it into a cloud. The long-delayed rain falls, the plain springs to life, and the cattle are saved.

READING STRATEGIES

PRE-READING

After showing the book cover and reading the title, point out Kenya on a world map to indicate where Kapiti Plain is located. Write plain on the chalkboard and explain that it means a flat stretch of land usually covered with tall grass. Then quickly show contrasting book illustrations—the plain as green and vibrant and the plain dry and brown. Explain that the latter shows the plain during a drought. Write the word drought on the chalkboard and explain that it means a long period of dry weather without rain. Invite volunteers to tell from the pictures what happens to the plain during a drought (the grass dies). Ask students to predict what happens to the animals that live on the plain during a drought (no grass to eat, no water to drink), and what must happen to end the drought (rain must fall). Then ask students to listen to the story to check their predictions.

WHILE READING

The story is told as a cumulative rhyme, along the lines of "The House That Jack Built." On the chalkboard, write the lines that end most stanzas, beginning with "To green-up the grass,/ all brown and dead." Rehearse ending lines with students, and invite students to say the lines aloud with you each time you come to them.

As students listen to the story and talk about the pictures, ask what-why-how questions that connect rainfall with the food and water needs of living things. For example: "What keeps the grass fresh and green?" "Why do the giraffes need the acacia trees?" "What do birds find to eat in the grass?" "What does the leopard eat?"

As another line of inquiry, discuss why Ki-pat's cattle don't leave the dry plain as the wild animals do. Help students to understand that the cattle are domesticated animals, depending on their owners to provide food and water. Students can compare the cattle to their own household pets.

After discussing the way Ki-pat brings rain to Kapiti Plain, invite students to tell whether this event is real or make-believe.

Then discuss what is real in the story. Talk about how many stories are made up of both real and make-believe events.

SCIENCE STRATEGIES

BUILDING THE SCIENCE CONNECTION

Introduce the activity by reviewing what happens when no rain falls on Kapiti Plain (the grass dies). Explain that the investigation will show students how plants such as grass take in water.

Set the two potted plants on a tray. Wrap aluminum foil or plastic wrap around the base of the stem of one plant, extending the wrap over the pot and onto the tray. The purpose is to collect runoff and to ensure that no water can reach the soil when the plant is watered.

Over a five-day period, ask students to water the soil with the same amount of water in the unwrapped plant and the leaves and stem of the wrapped plant.

After five days, the results will be obvious to your students: the plant whose soil was watered will be thriving, and the plant that got water only on leaves and stem will be drooping.

Briefly unpot the two plants and point out the roots on each. Ask students to feel the roots and determine which are wet and which are dry. Invite students to determine through which part of the plant the plant gets water to survive (through the roots) and how the roots get water (through the soil). Loop back to the story by asking how the soil on Kapiti Plain gets water (through rainfall). Firm up the concept by asking what would have happened if Ki-pat had gone out with a watering can and watered just the blades and blossoms on the grass of Kapiti Plain. Would the grass have continued to grow and thrive? Why or why not? Why did Ki-pat wish for rains to come? (to fill the soil with water for the roots of the grass)

EXTENDING THE SCIENCE CONNECTION

Students can use this activity to see how water moves upward from plant roots to the rest of the plant.

Stand the carrot—tip and any branch roots down—in the glass full of red-colored water. Let it stand for two days. After two days, help students cut the carrot crosswise. Ask students to point out the tubes in the carrot, discuss how they are colored red, and decide how they got that way (the water moved upwards through the carrot by capillary action).

Cut the carrot lengthwise so that students can trace how the water goes upward from the branch roots to the main root (the carrot itself) to the stem and leaves. Loop back to the story by asking students how a big plant like the giraffe's acacia tree gets water that enables the leaves on it to live. (rain to soil, soil to roots, root to stem [trunk], stem to leaves)

FOLLOW-UP ACTIVITIES

ORAL LANGUAGE: LISTENING AND ASKING

Invite a park ranger, natural history museum staffer, or another knowledgeable community resource person to visit your classroom and tell about the sources of water on which wild plants and animals of your region depend. Brainstorm a list of questions students hope the visitors can answer. Include the list in their written invitations. For example, how do birds get water in winter when everything is frozen? What happens to animals and plants when the water they use gets polluted? Has our region ever had droughts? If so, what has happened to the plants and animals? What can people do to help animals and plants get the water they need?

Write major questions on the chalkboard or on poster paper. Invite students to ask the visitor the questions. Ask students to listen for the responses so they can dictate a summary to you after the visitor has left. Conclude the activity

by asking each student to copy one question from the list and give the visitor's response in writing or in picture form. Compile the questions and answers in a folder for a table in your science center.

WRITING: USING THE BOOK AS A MODEL FOR A STORY

Invite students to work in cooperative learning groups to write and illustrate a book about what would happen if a drought hit your area. Introduce the activity by compiling a chalkboard list of plants and animals common to your region. Discuss the effects of a drought on these living things. Review how Ki-pat ended the drought.

Assign roles to the members of the groups. All members can discuss the plants and animals their book will tell about and imagine the hero or heroine who will end the drought through a magic device or action. One group member can note, in word or picture form, the sequences of action in the story. One group member can act as mediator as students choose a segment of the story to illustrate. After the illustrations are completed, two group members can help others write labels, captions, or sentences to go with their pictures. As the rest of the group works together to put the pictures in sequential order, two group members can make a front and back cover for the book.

Put the final stories on a table in your reading center. Invite small groups of students to read and discuss the stories and find one to act out for a small group of classmates.

ART: HAPPY UMBRELLAS

Kindergarten and Grade One students can use Activity Sheet 19 to summarize what they've learned about the importance of water to plants and animals. Introduce the activity by brainstorming a chalkboard list of living things in your area that benefit from rainfall. Then distribute copies of the Activity Sheet and discuss

From *Science & Stories*, Grades K–3, published by GoodYearBooks. Copyright © 1994 Hilarie N. Staton and Tara McCarthy.

the directions. After students have completed their umbrellas and cut them out, display their work around the classroom.

MATH: RAIN CHARTS

Invite interested third graders to refer to encyclopedias and almanacs to find the average amounts of precipitation (rain or snow) in your area throughout the year. Help your students interpret the data they find and to decide on visual ways of presenting it (bar graphs, tables, or illustrations). Discuss what "average" means, and encourage participating students to note weather figures in the local newspaper or on TV weather reports to see whether precipitation for a given month exceeds or falls short of the average.

GEOGRAPHY: MAPPING THE PLAINS

Provide interested students with large outline maps of North America. Ask them to use encyclopedias to find the North American Great Plains and color them in on their maps. Encourage students to list or draw within the boundaries of the Great Plains some examples of native plants and animals of the region. As students share their maps with the class, discuss how droughts affect farmers in the plains regions and how severe droughts and poor crops also affect food shoppers. You might also discuss any modern irrigation methods your class has been studying.

APPLYING THE SCIENCE CONCEPT:

☑ Invite students to develop their own projects for demonstrating what they have learned about how plants get water. Examples of projects include the following:

Project 1. Have students grow different kinds of plants from seed in starter flats and pots, carefully comparing the instructions on the seed packets as to how deep to plant and how often to water. Students should then follow the instructions to plant several different kinds of seeds and watch them grow.

Project 2. Have students grow an avocado plant from a pit suspended in water. This long-term project provides a "living cross-section" in which students can watch the development of branch roots, main roots, stem, and leaves.

Project 3. Students might also draw large labelled and colored cross-section diagrams of different kinds of plants in soil.

Bringing the Rain to Kapiti Plain

Name _____ Date _____

AN UMBRELLA FOR KI-PAT

DIRECTIONS

In each section of the umbrella, name or draw an animal or plant that needs rain. Then color and cut out the umbrella. Show it to your classmates.

From *Science & Stories*, Grades K-3, published by GoodYearBooks. Copyright © 1994 Hilarie N. Staton and Tara McCarthy.

LESSON 19

LITERATURE:
The Story of Jumping Mouse
John Steptoe (Mulberry Books, 1984)

SCIENCE:
Systems and Interactions

UNDERSTANDING:
Our senses enable us to get information.

INQUIRY SKILLS:
Observing, classifying

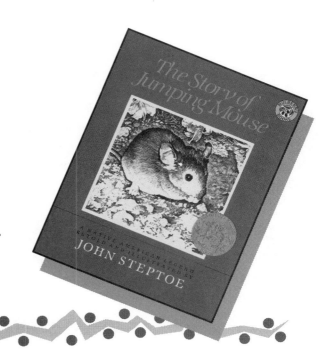

AHEAD *of* TIME

WHAT YOU'LL NEED

For Building the Science Connection
- variety of small objects that can be identified by touch, such as blocks, pencils, sandpaper, writing paper, toy car, and book
- cloth bag big enough to hold several objects and still allow students to handle the objects without looking
- 1" squares of blotter paper soaked in clove oil
- blindfolds
- tapes of sound effects
- a variety of foods for students to taste

For Extending the Science Connection
- earthworms and soil in a clear container

For Follow-Up Activities
- art materials for making books—construction paper, colored pencils or crayons, scissors, glue, paper punch, yarn or brads for binding pages (Writing)
- arrange with the school nurse to address the class (Health and Safety)
- recordings of classical music written to create specific word pictures (Music)

STORY SUMMARY

A young mouse is filled with dreams of the far-off land that is in the stories the old ones tell. He leaves home to follow his dream of seeing that land. At the edge of water, Magic Frog names him Jumping Mouse and gives him powerful hind legs. Jumping Mouse travels through the desert. At the end of his journey, he rests and becomes complacent in the company of a new friend—a fat, contented mouse. Suddenly, Jumping Mouse realizes he is in danger of giving up his dream in exchange for comfort and decides to continue his journey. When he goes to say good-by to the fat mouse, he finds the mouse has been eaten by a snake. Soon after, Jumping Mouse meets a poisoned bison and gives him a name (Eyes-of-a-Mouse) and his own sense of sight. The bison helps Jumping Mouse, who is now blind, reach the foot of the mountains safely. As Jumping Mouse travels toward the cool mountain breezes that he can smell, he remains confident that he can cope without his vision. The blind mouse soon smells a wolf, but is saddened when the wolf describes how he has lost hope because he has lost his sense of smell. Jumping Mouse renames the wolf Nose-of-a-Mouse as he gives him his own sense of smell. The wolf guides Jumping Mouse

through the mountains and then leaves him. The next morning Jumping Mouse realizes he has reached his goal—the far-off land—but cries when he realizes it will be hard for him to survive without either his sense of sight or smell. Magic Frog reappears and grants Jumping Mouse a new name—Eagle—a new body, and sharp new senses.

READING STRATEGIES
PRE-READING
Invite students to suggest some hopes and dreams a person might have. Encourage them to include simple items, such as reading better or getting a new toy, as well as more abstract ideas, such as peace on earth. Ask if all people have the same hopes and dreams. Encourage students to interview people about their hopes and dreams. Invite them to share their findings with the class.

With students, discuss the animals in the book (field mouse, bison, snake, frog, and wolf). Encourage students to identify different species of the same animal, such as different kinds of snakes. Invite them to compare how these snakes are alike and different in their looks, homes, and habits. Ask if all mice are the same. Encourage students to predict how the character in the title of the book, Jumping Mouse, might be different from the mice they've encountered. Invite students to pretend they are mice in the wild and to predict all the dangers they might encounter and the dreams they might have.

WHILE READING
Read the book to students. At appropriate places (such as the end of pages 3, 4, and 6) ask students to identify the problem or hardship encountered by Jumping Mouse. Have them predict how the problem will be solved. After you read the solution, ask students whether it was a "real life" solution or a "magic" one. If Jumping Mouse has a choice, ask students to predict which choice he'll make. After each decision is made, suggest students identify whether Jumping Mouse made a safe or risky decision. Encourage students to compare how Jumping Mouse acted when he lost the use of a sense to how the other animals acted when they lost the use of a sense.

After you have finished the book, have students identify what happened to each animal, including Jumping Mouse. Invite students to suggest words that describe Jumping Mouse, such as adventurous, dreamy, foolish, or kind.

SCIENCE STRATEGIES
BUILDING THE SCIENCE CONNECTION
Reread the story and have children locate places where Jumping Mouse used various senses. Discuss how each sense was used and how it helped Jumping Mouse learn about the world around him. Invite the class to create a list of descriptive words for each sense. Include words that describe things experienced through that specific sense. For touch, students might suggest *soft, smooth, bumpy, wet,* etc. These lists should be on the chalkboard or large paper so that students can add to them throughout the following activities.

Activity 1. Place several small items in a large bag. Have students put their hands into the bag and try to identify one object by touch, without seeing it.

You may want to introduce students to the objects before you place them in the bag. Or you can place several objects into the bag and have students describe the one they choose so that the class can guess what it is. Suggest students consult the class chart to find a variety of specific words to describe each object. Encourage students to add words to the chart as they describe a variety of items.

Activity 2. Invite students to identify one

96

From *Science & Stories, Grades K–3*, published by GoodYearBooks. Copyright © 1994 Hilarie N. Staton and Tara McCarthy.

another using only their senses of touch. A blindfolded student can touch another student's hair, face, and shoulders. Students describe what they learn and guess who the student is. If students have trouble with this activity, show them how you would make such a guess. You might say something like, "This person has long hair, so I know it's not Jesse, Rachel, or Mary Lou. They all have short hair. It might be Bernice, but she has curly hair. It must be Jackie. She has long straight hair and no bangs, just like this person."

Activity 3. Place several drops of clove oil on blotter paper and scatter the papers around an outdoor field. Have blindfolded students work with partners to find the papers by using their sense of smell only. The searcher moves about on his or her hands and knees to locate at least one paper by going toward the strong smell. The other partner acts as a lookout to keep the searcher safe. Then the partners switch roles.

Activity 4. Play records or tapes of sound effects or sounds made by common objects. Encourage students to identify what each is or represents. Partners can create their own sound effects tape and can ask another pair of students to identify the sounds without looking.

Activity 5. Encourage students to taste and smell several food dishes while blindfolded. They should try to identify a food by smell, and then guess again after they taste it. To make this a little easier or harder, have a partner describe how the food looks before the child makes his or her prediction. If you do unusual things, such as putting green food coloring in mashed potatoes, this can be an entertaining experience that shows how much we depend on sight for identification.

NOTE: Some students can become upset when they are blindfolded. Use less intimidating methods of blocking sight for these students, such as putting them behind a screen or allowing them to use their hands behind their back.

EXTENDING THE SCIENCE CONNECTION

Third-grade or interested students can manipulate the environment of an earthworm to see how it responds to various stimuli. Students can investigate whether the worms respond to direct touch, vibrations in the ground, strong smells (such as ammonia), or bright, direct light. Students can chart their findings and write a series of generalizations about how the earthworms use their senses. Even broader generalizations can be generated after students observe or do research on how other animals use their senses.

Related Stories. The lessons for *Whistle for Willie,* (page 6) and *Mandy* (page 100) include activities emphasizing the sense of hearing. *The Owl Moon* (page 10) lessons have activities in which students use more than one sense to make observations.

FOLLOW-UP ACTIVITIES
ORAL LANGUAGE: DESCRIBING ANIMALS

Show students animal pictures from picture books and science or nature magazines. Have them use the list of words they made in Building the Science Connection to describe the animals they see. Encourage them to use several specific rather than one general descriptive word. As you write the phrases, discuss the use of commas in lists. Encourage creative, even silly, sentences that use a variety of descriptive words from several senses.

Play a memory game with these descriptive phrases. One student gives a silly, descriptive phrase about an animal. The next student must repeat that one and add a new one. The next student must repeat all of those that went before, plus add a new one. Challenge students to remember as many phrases as possible. To make this easier, use picture clues to help students remember the order of the animals.

WRITING: A BOOK OF THE SENSES

Create a class book of the senses. Form five cooperative learning groups, one for each of the senses. Assign each group a different sense. Have the groups discuss everything they know about their senses and, if necessary, research for more information. Each group decides on a form for the pages in their book, such as a poem, sentences, or descriptions. Each group member is responsible for at least one page of that group's section.

After all sections are completed, have each group present its section to the class. The members can chorally read their pages while they show the appropriate picture. Join all the pages into a class book and place it in the class library to be reread by students.

WRITING: ANIMAL ANALOGIES

Introduce students to analogies, such as "rabbit fur is to soft as clam shell is to hard." Discuss different kinds of analogies, different things about animals that can be compared, different senses, and descriptive words. After the class has written several animal analogies together, have students form small teams of two or three students. Encourage each team to write three or four animal analogies. Allow each team to share one analogy with the class and collect the rest.

Use the collected analogies in an activity sheet. Leave blank one of the four components in each analogy. If this is the first time students have written or completed analogies, you may need to edit their analogies or provide multiple choices for them to use in completing the analogies. Students can work together to complete worksheets and then share their answers with the class. Encourage them to explain how and why they made the choices they did.

HEALTH AND SAFETY: TAKING CARE OF YOUR SENSES

Invite the school nurse to speak to the class about the importance of their senses and ways to care for them. Divide the class into cooperative learning groups and have each group choose a different way to care for a sense, such as wearing glasses, using potholders, or keeping the sound low on earphones. Each group makes a poster or writes a skit to promote its concern. Display the posters around the school and encourage groups to present their skits to other classes.

MUSIC: MUSICAL PICTURES

There are several pieces of classical music that were written to create specific pictures. Some of these pieces are: Ravel's *Jeux d'eau* (*Fountains*), Debussy's prelude *Fireworks,* or Moussorgsky's *Pictures at an Exhibition.* Play a few of these for students. Tell them the composer is trying to paint a picture in their minds. As they listen to the music, ask them to try to determine what picture the composer is trying to draw. Invite them to draw the pictures the music creates in their mind.

APPLYING THE SCIENCE CONCEPT:

☑ Distribute Activity Sheet 19 to students. Tell them they must use their senses to understand the scene on this sheet. Under the picture are five symbols, one for each sense. Identify the symbols for students and make the connection to the specific sense. Then have students draw lines to items in the scene to the sense they'd use to understand it. Invite them to match some items to more than one sense.

From *Science & Stories*, Grades K-3, published by GoodYearBooks. Copyright © 1994 Hilarie N. Staton and Tara McCarthy.

The Story of Jumping Mouse

Name _____   Date _____

GREAT-GRANDMA'S KITCHEN

DIRECTIONS

How would you use your senses to learn about this scene? For each sense below, draw a line to three things you could learn about by using that sense.

EAR
HEARING

EYE
SIGHT

HAND
TOUCH

MOUTH
TASTE

NOSE
SMELL

LITERATURE:
Mandy
Barbara D. Booth (Lothrop, Lee & Shepard Books, 1991)

SCIENCE:
Systems and Interactions

UNDERSTANDING:
Sound is made by vibrations that travel through matter.

INQUIRY SKILLS:
Observing, recording data, generalizing, inferring, manipulating materials

AHEAD *of* TIME

WHAT YOU'LL NEED

For Building the Science Connection
- large rubber bands
- stringed instruments, such as guitar, violin, banjo
- spatula with metal blade
- drum
- fine sand
- large picture of inner ear
- variety of objects to make sounds, such as metal toy, pencil, lunch box, paper bag

For Extending the Science Connection
- wooden box
- cotton balls

For Follow-Up Activities
- arrange for a hearing-impaired person to address the class (Oral Language)
- pictures of interiors and exteriors of buildings around your community (Social Studies/Visual Memory)
- scissors, glue, crayons or colored pencils for Activity Sheet 20 (Applying the Science Concept)

STORY SUMMARY

Mandy and her grandmother enjoy doing everyday things like baking cookies. Everything is done in a little different way, however, because Mandy is hearing impaired. She feels the vibrations of the radio instead of hearing the music. She judges the baking cookies by where the smell reaches instead of by hearing the kitchen timer. Mandy is often confused by phrases people use. She once tried to stuff a marshmallow in her ear when someone described her mother's voice as soft and sweet. One day, Mandy and her grandmother go for a walk in the woods. Her grandmother becomes distressed when she loses a pin that is very precious to her. They search for the pin, but do not find it and must return to the house to fix dinner. Then, in spite of her fears of storms and the dark, Mandy ventures out on her own to search for her grandmother's pin. She finds the pin when she falls and the light from her flashlight strikes it. Her reward is the pleasure on her grandmother's face when she returns the pin to her.

READING STRATEGIES

PRE-READING

Write the term "Hearing World" on the chalkboard. Invite students to tell what they think it means. Ask them who they think belongs to the hearing world and who doesn't. Invite them to suggest problems that people who are hearing impaired have in a hearing world. Encourage students to suggest everyday things that hearing impaired people are unable to use or enjoy, such as radios, doorbells, car horns, etc. Invite students to suggest ways that hearing-impaired people might get the same information that we get from sound, like flashing lights for a doorbell. Encourage students to identify or invent solutions for the problems they've identified.

Write the following questions on the chalkboard. Have students consider these questions as they listen to the story.

- How does Mandy get the information that other people get through their hearing? (There are many possible answers. Examples might include: the cookies' smell, watching people's lips and faces, and feeling the radio's sound through the floor.)
- What misunderstandings does Mandy have about the world because she cannot hear? (There are many possible answers, including the radio's relationship to dancing, branches making loud noises because they are big, and outside noises hurting people's ears.)
- How are Mandy's actions and feelings like those of other children? (There are many possible answers. Students might mention liking to bake with her grandmother, loving her grandmother and grandfather, and wanting her grandmother to be happy.)

WHILE READING

Read the book to students. Stop at various points and consider the answers to the above questions. After you complete the book, encourage students to discuss incidents that illustrate their thoughts on each question.

SCIENCE STRATEGIES

BUILDING THE SCIENCE CONNECTION

Activity 1. Reread the third page of text in the book. Emphasize the section where Mandy talks about feeling the sound of the radio through the floor. Invite students to share times when they felt sounds. Suggest they construct a statement (a hypothesis) about what was happening during these incidents.

Activity 2. Divide the class into small groups. Have each group perform one or more of the following activities and record what they see, hear, and feel. (a) Fasten a rubber band to a stationary object, such as a doorknob. Pull it taut and pluck it. (b) Pluck the strings of a stringed instrument. Touch the strings lightly as it is played. (c) Hold a spatula blade flat on the desk and extend the handle over the desk's edge. Pull the handle down and then let it go. (d) Create a grass or paper whistle by holding it taut between two fingers and blowing hard. (e) Place fine sand or salt on a drumhead and tap it gently.

Allow each group to share its observations with the class. Create a class chart of what groups observed and develop a definition of vibrations (something moving back and forth or up and down). Encourage students to make the generalization that vibrations create sound.

Activity 3. Display a picture of an inner ear. Have students identify the eardrum by its likeness to a drum. Encourage them to apply their generalization about vibrations and sound to the eardrum and to predict what happens to the eardrum when a sound reaches it. (It vibrates.) Point out the small bones behind the eardrum and ask students what they think happens to them when the eardrum vibrates. (They vibrate too.) Help students draw the generalization that sound travels by vibrations moving from one thing to the next. Draw a diagram that illustrates the path from a common sound-producing object to the inner ear.

Activity 4. Divide students into small groups. Give each group several objects made of various materials (or have them choose various common objects). Invite them to make each object vibrate and to describe the sound each makes in as many ways as possible (loud, soft, deep, high) and to describe how long the sound persists. Assign a recorder for each group to keep track of the group's findings. Assign a presenter to share the group's findings with the class.

EXTENDING THE SCIENCE CONNECTION
Activity. Third-grade, interested, or more able students can experiment with materials that soften or deaden sound. A student can place a rubber band around a wooden box and pluck it. By filling the box with things like water, paper, sand, cloth, or cotton balls and then plucking the rubber band again, students can determine which materials deaden sound. The sound will change according to the material used in the box. Students can develop scales that indicate which materials deaden sound and which enhance it. Students can compare these scales to identify the best materials for deadening sound and the best materials for carrying sound.

Further Reading. Interested students can learn about speech reading, sign language, and other ways severely hearing impaired people compensate for their hearing loss. Other children's literature that deals with hearing-impaired people includes L. Aseltine and E. Mueller's book *I'm Deaf and It's Okay,* L. Guccione's book *Tell Me How the Wind Sounds,* and M. Riskind's book *Apple Is My Sign.* For information, students can write to the Alexander Graham Bell Association for the Deaf (3417 Volta Place, NW, Washington, DC 20007) or the American Society for Deaf Children (814 Thayer Avenue, Silver Springs, MD 20910).

You will find other activities that relate to the senses under the following books: *Whistle for Willie* (page 6) and *The Jumping Mouse* (page 95).

FOLLOW-UP ACTIVITIES
ORAL LANGUAGE: COMMUNICATION WITHOUT SPEECH
Invite students to suggest ways they would communicate if they couldn't speak. Suggest they play charades and act out simple sentences without speaking. Write simple action sentences that are easy to act out (Tio plays the piano) and simple, non-action sentences that are more difficult to act out (The pencil is blue). As the students play, help them draw the conclusions that some things are easier to say without speech and that it takes much longer to convey information without speech.

Invite a hearing-impaired student or adult to talk to the class about what they hear, what part vibrations play in their hearing process, how they compensate for their loss, and ways they communicate. Before the speaker arrives, help the class devise an appropriate way to convey a welcome to this person, such as using the sign for hello. Be sure that the speaker uses whatever procedure you choose.

WRITING: HEAR OUR RECOMMENDATIONS
Present students with this hypothetical problem: a hearing impaired student will be joining their class. They need to develop ways to communicate with the student. Divide the class into small groups. Have each group think of ways that they could make communications with the new student easier. Each group creates a plan involving several methods and each member investigates one method and its pros and cons. If more than one student is examining the same method, expert groups can form.

Have each group member write a paragraph describing his or her method and share it with the group. The group then re-evaluates the methods included in its plan to see how each would fit into the classroom. As a final presentation, students can write a letter to the principal (or to the new hearing-impaired student) with

From *Science & Stories*, Grades K-3, published by GoodYearBooks. Copyright © 1994 Hilarie N. Staton and Tara McCarthy.

their final recommendations. Each group can develop a portfolio that includes their communication ideas, each member's paragraph (and maybe research notes), notes on the group's conclusions, and the group's final letter. You can give both group and individual grades for the work in the portfolio.

SOCIAL STUDIES/VISUAL MEMORY: WHERE NEXT?

Students in kindergarten or first grade can pretend they are not able to use their hearing but have errands to do in the community. Display and discuss pictures of the inside or outside of a local place, such as a bank, the library, or a grocery store. Explain that you will show them pictures of these places. Display three to six pictures for a limited amount of time. Now have students "do their errands" by picking the pictures you displayed out of a larger set of pictures or by writing a list of where they have to go. If students are skilled at this, you can increase the number of places or require that the "errands" be done in a specific order.

LITERATURE: FIGURING OUT FIGURATIVE LANGUAGE

Reread *Mandy* and have students listen for phrases that Mandy has trouble understanding, such as "a soft and sweet voice." Tell students that many people have trouble understanding these types of phrases, especially if they have hearing problems or are learning a new language. Invite students to suggest ways people can misinterpret a few common phrases, such as "raining cats and dogs." Create a class list of phrases that people misunderstand.

Read other books that introduce figurative language, such as James Cox's *Put Your Foot In Your Mouth and Other Silly Sayings,* Fred Gwynne's *A Chocolate Moose for Dinner,* Ann Nevins' *From the Horse's Mouth,* or Peggy Parish's *Amelia Bedelia.* Add new phrases to the class list.

Have each student choose a phrase and create an illustration that shows a silly way the phrase can be misinterpreted. Students might choose to show dogs and cats raining from the sky, or Mandy's mother with marshmallows coming out of her mouth. Invite students to present their pictures to the class, to explain them, and to explain the accepted meaning of the phrases they are illustrating. You can collect all the illustrated phrases in a class book.

APPLYING THE SCIENCE CONCEPT:

☑ Distribute Activity Sheet 20 to students. Identify the pictures at the bottom of the page (drumsticks, a drum, and an ear). Point out that the wavy lines are used to represent sound vibrations. Tell students they are to create a diagram that shows how the sound travels from the drumsticks to the ear. Instruct students to cut out the pictures, organize them in sequence, and add wavy lines between appropriate pictures. Have students draw a star any place that vibrations occur. The final diagram should look something like the one below.

Mandy

Name _____ Date _____

LISTEN TO THE MUSIC

DIRECTIONS

Cut out the pictures below. Arrange them to show how sound is made and travels. Use wavy lines to show how vibrations move through the air. Draw a star (*) on every place vibrations can be felt.

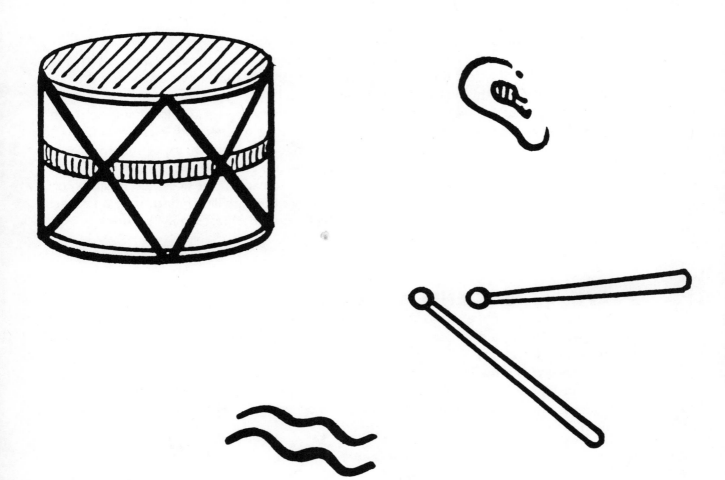

From *Science & Stories*, Grades K–3, published by GoodYearBooks. Copyright © 1994 Hilarie N. Staton and Tara McCarthy.

LITERATURE:
The Magic School Bus Inside the Human Body
Joanna Cole (Scholastic, 1989)

SCIENCE:
Systems and Interactions

UNDERSTANDING:
Humans have properties that enable them to meet their needs.

INQUIRY SKILLS:
Creating models, classifying, manipulating materials, observing, recording data

AHEAD *of* TIME

WHAT YOU'LL NEED

For Pre-Reading
- piece of paper, large enough to trace a student's body
- crayon or marker
- masking tape

For Building the Science Connection
- reference books or science textbooks with information on organs of the human body
- art materials for making cutouts and drawing diagrams—construction paper, scissors, crayons, colored pencils, or markers

For Extending the Science Connection
- prepared slides of cells
- microscope

For Follow-Up Activities
- art materials for making body-systems map and picture cards—large paper with body outline, crayons, colored pencils or markers, small toy school bus, large index cards (Oral Language)
- blank or graph paper, ruler, construction paper, pencils or crayons for drawing charts (Math)

STORY SUMMARY

Ms. Frizzle's class leaves for a trip to the science museum, but the bus, holding everyone but Arnold, shrinks and is swallowed by Arnold. As Arnold makes his way back to school, the bus travels through Arnold's stomach, small intestine, blood stream, lungs, brain, spinal cord, and muscles. During this trip, Ms. Frizzle explains how each system works. The students leave the bus when it is attacked by white blood cells, but they continue through Arnold's body. They reboard the bus just before it is sneezed out by Arnold, who is standing in front of the school. Also included throughout the book are

student science reports on different parts, systems, and terms along with illustrations that explain the concepts. At the very end of the book is a short true-false test.

READING STRATEGIES
PRE-READING

Invite a volunteer to lie down on a large sheet of paper and trace that student's outline. Tape the blank outline to the chalkboard. Have students suggest what could be added to make this a more complete picture of the student. Encourage students to list what they would draw if they were going to show what is inside a person. Keep a list of all of their suggestions.

Explain that inside the human body are several important systems. Encourage students to list the systems they know. Be sure the following are on the list: digestive system, circulatory system, respiratory system, nervous system, muscular system, and skeletal system. Write each system as a category heading on the chalkboard or a large sheet of paper. Tell students that, like other systems, each of the body's systems is made up of many separate parts. Invite students to write names of body parts they know under the appropriate category. Suggest they keep another list of parts they know are in the body but are not sure what system the part belongs to. Encourage students to draw on their prior knowledge from science and health to do this categorization.

Invite students to recall prior knowledge of cells, or define the term *cell* for them. (A cell is the smallest unit of structure of which all plants and animals are composed.) Compare a cell to a building brick. Ask students how they think cells relate to the systems in the human body. (Different types of cells make up each part of a system.) The detail and length covered by this activity will depend on students' prior knowledge of cells and your goals for the lesson.

Display the book and tell students that there is a lot of factual information in among the

fantasy. They must carefully determine which is which. Remind students to listen for the terms on their chart so they can verify, correct, or place terms under the correct system.

WHILE READING

As you read the book to students, stop after each page to discuss the text, the word balloons, reports, side bars, and illustrations, and to identify what is real and what is fantasy. Encourage students to tie what they are reading to their prior knowledge. Invite students to add to or rearrange the vocabulary chart as they encounter new terms.

SCIENCE STRATEGIES
BUILDING THE SCIENCE CONNECTION

Review the systems discussed in the book and relate them to the vocabulary chart students have created. Invite volunteers to summarize the information for each system.

Using cooperative learning groups, have each group study one system. Group members create cutouts of their system, including the organs that are part of it. The systems can be placed on the human outline made during the pre-reading activity. (There is a sample of the finished activity at the end of the book.) Each group can also create a diagram of its system and its functions. For instance, a diagram for the circulatory system can show how the blood circulates to the heart, lungs, and various other parts of the body before returning to the heart.

EXTENDING THE SCIENCE CONNECTION
Activity 1. Third graders or more able or interested students can do a "jigsaw" cooperative learning activity. All groups have the same system and each member of the group chooses a different organ within that system. Students form expert groups by meeting with members of other groups who are studying the same organ. These expert groups investigate their

From *Science & Stories*, Grades K-3, published by GoodYearBooks. Copyright © 1994 Hilarie N. Staton and Tara McCarthy.

organs, including how they fit into the system, how they work, what is necessary to keep them healthy, and problems that could develop with them. They can also create an activity to help explain how the organ works. For example, students studying the stomach can put vinegar on bread to show what stomach acid does to food. Students then return to their first group to teach the rest of the groups about the organ they studied.

Activity 2. Third graders or interested students can learn more about cells. They can locate, examine, and draw cells of different types from both plants and animals. For example, they can examine prepared slides of potato cells, onion cells, or lettuce cells under a microscope, draw what they see, and share their observations with other students.

FOLLOW-UP ACTIVITIES

ORAL LANGUAGE: FOLLOWING DIRECTIONS

Use the class body outline with its exposed systems as a map. Have volunteers recall the route of the Magic School Bus through Arnold's body, while other volunteers move a small toy school bus through the body. After students have followed the book's journey, invite them to meet in small groups and create their own journeys. They can write directions for their trips through the body. Remind students to use appropriate direction words such as *under, through,* and *between.* Each group reads its directions to another group, which moves the school bus according to the directions given.

ORAL LANGUAGE: BODY JEOPARDY

Using the class body outline, discuss each system, its function, parts, and where it is in relation to the body's other organs and systems. Have each student make a card with an illustration or word representing an organ or system on one side. Assign a specific number of points to each card and place that number on the other side. The easier systems should be worth

fewer points than the harder to identify organs. Thumbtack these cards, picture down, onto a bulletin board. Organize the cards by general areas or place them in random order.

Divide the class into two or three cooperative teams to play "Body Jeopardy." Each team takes a turn, with one team member choosing a card. The group members turn the chosen card over. Then the team confers to identify the picture or define the word. The answers should be given as complete sentences (or questions) that name the item and give at least one fact about it. These facts might include the system an organ is part of, what an organ or system's purpose is, or where it is located. Teams get the assigned points for correct answers. If they give an incorrect answer or don't know the answer, another team gets a chance to answer it and win the points. Play rotates to each team, so all get a turn to choose and answer. The winning team is the one with the most points when the cards are gone.

WRITING: BODY REPORTS

For each of the terms on their original vocabulary chart, invite students to write a short report of one or two paragraphs, like those in *The Magic School Bus Inside the Human Body.* For reference, they can consult *The Magic School Bus* and at least two other sources (such as their science books). Suggest they create illustrations to go with their reports. Display their reports and illustrations or join them together into a class body book. Invite students to share their reports with the whole class.

MATH: CREATING AND READING CHARTS

Invite groups of students to research statistics about a system and create a chart with that information. They should also devise questions about the chart. For example, students might investigate digestion and create a chart that shows where food is every 15 minutes for three hours after it is eaten. Their questions can be about the information found on their chart, such as "Where is pizza 30 minutes after you eat it?" Encourage groups to switch charts and questions to test their knowledge. Allow children to revise their charts and questions as needed. After the charts and questions are revised, place them in a math learning center or on a bulletin board for others to try.

APPLYING THE SCIENCE CONCEPT

☑ Distribute Activity Sheet 21 to students. Have them, individually or in teams, read the "Who Am I?" questions, figure out the correct organs or systems, and then write the correct labels on the diagram of the body.

The Magic School Bus Inside the Human Body

Name _____ Date _____

WHO AM I?

DIRECTIONS

Write the answer to each "Who Am I?" question in the answer space. Write the organs you use on the body outline below.

muscles   lungs   stomach   **brain   heart**

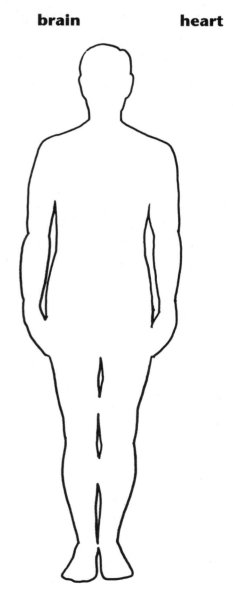

1. We help air get into your body. We fill and empty as you breathe. Who are we?

   _____

2. I am where you think. I help you decide When to move your arm. Who am I?

   _____

3. I get very full when you eat too much. I have to work hard to digest food you don't chew. Who am I?

   _____

4. We are all over your body. We help you move, stand, sit, and eat. We work together. We take orders from your brains. Who are we?

   _____

5. I am a pump that sends blood all over your body. All blood passes through me on its way to the arteries. Who am I?

   _____

LITERATURE:
Letting Swift River Go
Jane Yolen (Little, Brown, 1992)

SCIENCE:
Methods of Observation

UNDERSTANDING:
People solve problems through given processes.

INQUIRY SKILLS:
Observing, identifying variables, recording data, interpreting data, generalizing, inferring

AHEAD *of* TIME

WHAT YOU'LL NEED

For Building the Science Connection
• a class chart of the problem-solving steps
• water in a clear container

For Follow-Up Activities
• materials for making a class newspaper —paper, drawing materials (Writing)
• local, state, United States, or world maps (Geography)

STORY SUMMARY

Six-year-old Sally Jane lives in the Massachusetts countryside. She walks to school by herself. She fishes, plays mumblety-peg, and picnics with friends. On summer nights, she and her friend listen to noises and watch shadows and fireflies as they sleep outdoors. Her family harvests ice in winter and taps maple trees in the spring. Then, when the adults begin going to town meetings, everything changes. Men from Boston tell local residents that the people in Boston need the water from the valley. Soon, workers come in and move the cemetery. They cut down all the trees and move or demolish the buildings in the valley. The people move away and machines move in. Sally Jane's family moves to a smaller, warmer house in a small town nearby. The people from Boston build dams and then flood the valley with water. The water covers all the Swift River towns. The adult Sally Jane and her father return to the Quablin Reservoir. As they float on the water, he points out where landmarks once stood. Finally Sally Jane accepts the new beauty people created over the old.

From *Science & Stories*, Grades K-3, published by GoodYearBooks. Copyright © 1994 Hilarie N. Staton and Tara McCarthy.

READING STRATEGIES

PRE-READING

If students are unfamiliar with the problem-solving process, introduce its steps on a chart like the following:

Problem Solving

Step 1. What is the problem?

Step 2. What are all the ways it could be solved?

Step 3. Which might be the best solutions?

Step 4. What are the consequences of each of those solutions?

Step 5. Which solution will be tried first?

Encourage students to become good problem solvers by following these steps carefully. Create several simple, hypothetical problems and talk through the problem-solving process. You might consider problems such as these:

(a) You must choose one of your three best friends to go on a trip with you. You don't want to upset any of them. What will you do?

(b) Your mother brings home your favorite food, but says you have to wait and share it with your sister when she comes home. You know your sister will try to eat it all. What will you do?

(c) The class is on a field trip to the woods. You are getting ready to have lunch when everyone realizes that animals have gotten into the bus and eaten most of the lunches. There are 20 students, but only four sandwiches left.

Go through the problem-solving process with students. Model the way you think and make your decisions. Refer to the chart often. Emphasize simple problem statements for step 1, creative brainstorming (develop many ideas, even outrageous ones) for step 2, realistic evaluation for step 3, prediction of both good and bad consequences for step 4, and evaluation for step 5 (which has the best trade-offs).

Hold up a clear container that has some water in it. Invite students to think of all the possible uses for water, including water in streams, lakes, and homes. During the discussion, encourage students to describe how city people use water and to identify the water problems a growing city might have. (People use more water than is available.) With students, list suggestions about what a city might do to solve each problem. Introduce the word *reservoir* and discuss its meaning. (A body of water, either a natural or artificial lake, collected and stored for future use.) Tell students that they are going to hear the story of what happened when the people of Boston needed more water.

WHILE READING

Read the book to students. Because many phrases and objects might be unfamiliar to most students, help students use context to determine meaning. Suggest they use the pictures, capital letters, or words around the unknown word to help them understand a word's meaning or its importance in the story. For instance, you might demonstrate how you figure out from the context that mumblety-peg is a game. (The verb *played* is used with it.)

While you are reading, have students identify problems that are part of the story. These might include: Boston needed more water, the local people had to move. Encourage students to identify the solutions to each problem.

SCIENCE STRATEGIES

BUILDING THE SCIENCE CONNECTION

Review with students the problem-solving process. Discuss how the process can be applied to various social, academic, and scientific situations. Divide the class into small groups. Have each group develop a problem situation. You can limit problems to science situations in which students have a background (such as why a plant is losing its leaves or how we will move a big boulder). Or you can broaden the categories to social or academic situations (such as what do you do if you get lost in a store or if you can't do a math problem). Have each group create a skit of its problem situation and then present it to the class. For one or two presentations, invite the class to go through the problem-solving process with you. Encourage the groups to use the process with another problem and share their results with the class.

EXTENDING THE SCIENCE CONNECTION

Activity 1. Third-grade or interested students can investigate more about water, where it comes from, and how it gets to their homes. Joanna Cole's book *The Magic School Bus at the Waterworks* describes ways technology solves problems. Students can also investigate how cities like Boston or New York City can be by the ocean and still run out of water for its people to use (salt verses fresh water). Invite students to present their findings in murals or written reports.

Activity 2. Students interested in technological solutions can review newspapers and news broadcasts for modern problems and the ways science is solving them. They can create a science problem-solving bulletin board with their summaries of these problems and illustrations of both scientists' and their own possible solutions.

FOLLOW-UP ACTIVITIES

ORAL LANGUAGE: SOLVING THE PROBLEMS OF SWIFT RIVER

Reread the story and review the problems that students have identified. Form cooperative learning groups and assign each group a person or group from the book (for example, the people in Boston, a local farmer, Sally Jane's family). After groups identify one problem their characters have, they use the problem-solving process to come up with alternate solutions for that

problem. Reread the book to the class, but stop at appropriate spots and have the group that studied the pertinent problem present its ideas on alternate solutions.

WRITING: THE NEWS FROM SWIFT RIVER

Have students, individually or in pairs, write newspaper articles covering events that happened in the Swift River area. Some might write about life before the reservoir. Others might write about the town meetings (from various viewpoints), the demolition, or fishing on the new reservoir. Collect these into a Swift River newspaper.

GEOGRAPHY: WATER, WATER, EVERYWHERE

Divide the class into small groups. Give each group at least one state, U.S., or world map that uses blue only for water. Have the group locate all the blue areas and identify their names. Help them draw the conclusion that blue represents bodies of water and then to categorize the types of bodies of water they find such as rivers, lakes, and oceans. If they are using state or local maps, have them locate reservoirs and hypothesize about where the water goes. Encourage students to create a local water map. Have them label important bodies of water and identify the route their local drinking water takes. Invite students to write descriptions of that route from the viewpoint of a drop of water.

SOCIAL STUDIES/HISTORY: PROBLEMS OF THE PAST

Create a list of problems faced in your local area throughout its history. This could include disastrous fires, poor travel conditions, lack of shelters, or battles fought. Choose one problem and use the problem solving process with students to identify possible solutions and the effects each solution would have had on the

From *Science & Stories*, Grades K–3, published by GoodYearBooks. Copyright © 1994 Hilarie N. Staton and Tara McCarthy.

local environment and people. Then investigate how the problem was solved and the effect that solution had. Encourage students to discuss whether they would have chosen that solution and to give reasons why or why not. Small groups can consider other historical problems and illustrate their recommended and actual solutions. These can be presented to the class or posted on a historical bulletin board.

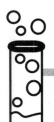

APPLYING THE SCIENCE CONCEPT:

✓ Distribute Activity Sheet 22 to students. Have students examine the picture on the activity sheet. Then have students complete the problem-solving process either individually or in small groups. Encourage students to share what they did for each step. Invite alternative answers to each question.

Letting Swift River Go

Name _____ Date _____

WHAT TO DO?

DIRECTIONS
Maria needs to move this machine from the table to the garage. It is very heavy.

Step 1. What is Maria's problem?

Step 2. What are all the ways she could possibly solve her problem?

Step 3. Which might be the best solutions?

Step 4. What are the consequences of each of these solutions?

Step 5. Which solution do you think Maria should try first and why?

Step 6. Write a paragraph that tells how Maria carries out the solution you've chosen.

From *Science & Stories, Grades K-3*, published by GoodYearBooks. Copyright © 1994 Hilarie N. Staton and Tara McCarthy.

LITERATURE:
Heron Street
Ann Turner (Harper & Row, 1989)

SCIENCE:
Patterns of Change

UNDERSTANDING:
Change in one part of the environment causes changes in other parts.

INQUIRY SKILLS:
Observing, identifying variables, recording data, interpreting data, generalizing, inferring

AHEAD *of* TIME

WHAT YOU'LL NEED

For Building the Science Connection
Plan a class field trip to a relatively intact natural area near you such as a pond, woods, or field. Students will need the following:

- copies of Activity Sheet 23, mounted on cardboard for durability
- extra paper
- drawing and coloring materials
- if possible, small tape recorders each to be shared by two or three students
- hand lenses
- sturdy bags or knapsacks for carrying the supplies above
- (optional) camera

STORY SUMMARY

The book presents the history of a seaside marsh and the animals and plants that have lived there from the time before humans arrived to modern times. The vivid pictures and simple text show how human activities and technology reshape environments to serve the exclusive needs of people. The original habitat is so completely altered that most of the original inhabitants can no longer live there.

READING STRATEGIES

PRE-READING

Start by easing students into a basic understanding of what a habitat is. After showing the book cover and reading the title, explain that the story is about a neighborhood. Then show the frontispiece (the illustration facing the title page) and have students point out the familiar features they associate with a neighborhood—houses, streets, lawns. Then show the first two pictures in the story and tell students that these, too, are pictures of a neighborhood—a neighborhood where wild animals and plants live. Explain that scientists use the word *habitat* when talking about animal and plant neighborhoods. Discuss the things animals need in their habitats, or neighborhoods: food, water, shelter, space; ask if humans need these too. Then ask students to listen to the story to find out how

the animals' and plants' habitats change and what happens to the plants and animals as a result.

WHILE READING

Much of the theme of the story is presented through sound words, such as the recurring "Shhh-hello, hsss-hello" of the tall grass in the wind, the "honk" of the herons, and the sounds made by people, their livestock, and their tools and machines. As you read, emphasize these words to indicate how human sounds gradually take over the environment. From time to time, invite a student to reread a page with you and say the sound-word independently. Conclude the story by discussing why the animals left and why so little tall grass remains to whisper in the wind. Make sure students understand that in the human neighborhood there is nothing left for the animals to eat and no place for them to find shelter and move about freely.

SCIENCE STRATEGIES

BUILDING THE SCIENCE CONNECTION
Before the field trip. Explain that the purpose of the field trip is to find many different kinds of plants and animals in their natural habitat, or neighborhood, and to record their findings. Distribute the mounted Activity Sheets and explain and discuss what students are to look for and draw. If you are taking hand lenses and tape recorders, explain how they are to be used; the first for close-up looks, the second to record any natural sounds students hear, such as the whispering of wind in the grass, the calls of birds, or the chirps of crickets. Also develop with the class a short list of "courtesy rules" to follow when they explore a neighborhood that belongs to other beings. For example: (a) Walk softly; (b) Don't yell; (c) Don't touch without an adult's permission; (d) Don't take things out of their natural setting. They don't belong to you.

During the field trip. As both a safety precaution and a learning strategy, have students work with partners as they explore the site and look for examples to draw on their Activity Sheets. From time to time, bring the class together to review students' findings and to share information about where to look for specific items. Try to make sure that each student returns to school with a completed Activity Sheet.

Back in the classroom. Invite students to work in small groups to show and discuss their Activity Sheets. Then display the sheets on a bulletin board under the banner "A Habitat: What We Found at (name of place you visited)." You will use this display as the basis for the Oral Language Activity that follows. If students have made tape recordings of sounds heard in the habitat, invite them to play the tapes and have other students guess what made the sounds.

EXTENDING THE SCIENCE CONNECTION

☑ Invite small groups of students to discuss their own habitats and then draw picture maps of them. Explain that their picture maps should show the following: where they get food; where they get water; where they find shelter; spaces through which they move; living things (other than humans) that are in their habitats.

Ask groups to show their picture maps to the class. Encourage the class to discuss the likenesses and differences in the pictures. Exhibit the maps on a table near the bulletin board display described above.

FOLLOW-UP ACTIVITIES

ORAL LANGUAGE: TALKING AND THINKING ABOUT CHANGES
Introduce the activity by reviewing what happened to the habitat of animals and plants in *Heron Street*. What specific human activities made the marsh no longer a good home for the original inhabitants?

Refer students to their posted results from

From *Science & Stories*, Grades K-3, published by GoodYearBooks. Copyright © 1994 Hilarie N. Staton and Tara McCarthy.

the field trip. Pose these problems and questions for them to discuss:

1. Suppose you decide to build a tree house in the habitat we visited. Would anything that lives there be disturbed? If so, what?

2. Suppose people decided to cut down a few trees in the habitat, mow the grass, move some rocks, and make a park. Would anything that lives there be disturbed? How?

3. Suppose people decided to build many houses and roads in the habitat. Tell about some things that would happen to the animals and plants that live there now.

As students discuss this last problem, you many find that many of them believe that the animals simply "go someplace else to live." In fact, of course, there most often is no "someplace else," and many species dwindle to the verge of extinction. It's a fact that children have a right to know, yet it can upset them emotionally—mainly because young children often feel helpless to counteract human encroachments on and destruction of other living things. So you may wish to temper the bad news with some bits of good news that may help children feel empowered. Some examples of "good news" are:

- Point out that many animals, such as deer, raccoons, chipmunks, and squirrels, have learned to share human habitats. For example, the borders of farmland and forests are favorite feeding grounds for deer.
- Bluebirds were once threatened with extinction because their nesting bushes and trees were destroyed as housing projects were built. But the bluebird is making a comeback now, because caring people built "bluebird trails" across the nation, setting up special bluebird houses in places where bluebirds like to nest.
- Many kinds of whales were once threatened with extinction. Children all over the world participated in a letter-writing campaign, writing to the heads of nations that allowed whale hunting. As a result of the campaign, the threatened whales are now a protected species.

You might conclude this activity by discussing threatened animals that students have heard about, such as wolves in Alaska and coral reefs in the Caribbean and Atlantic. Help interested students develop and carry out ideas for campaigns of their own that might contribute to the preservation of some threatened animal or plant in your own area.

WRITING: A GROUP POEM

Invite students to work in groups to write three-stanza poems about habitats. The first stanza should tell about the habitat they visited on the field trip. The second stanza should tell about their own habitats, as shown in the picture maps they made for Extending the Science Connection. The third stanza should be a brief paragraph summarizing how the habitats are alike or different.

Introduce the activity by asking the class to brainstorm a chalkboard list of vivid words and phrases that describe the things they saw on their field trip. They might list fluffy flowers no bigger than my thumb, a gray rock covered with green moss, a bird looking down at me from a tall tree, or the sound of a cricket. Then brainstorm in the same way for words and phrases based on the picture maps, such as houses all scrunched together, a leafy park to play in, or the store where I buy muffins and milk. Stress that poems need not rhyme, and that the important thing is to fill the poem with words and phrases that help the listener or reader see things in the mind's eye. Each stanza should be written in final form on a large sheet of poster paper, "Big Book" style. Provide scrap paper for drafts and practice.

As students form their writing groups, suggest that they assign the following roles: two scribes who take turns recording the lines for the first two stanzas on scrap paper; two editors to help other writers revise and edit their lines; and a moderator to assign each group member the writing and illustrating of a line in both stanzas on the final poster paper.

Suggest that group members work together to compose the final, summing-up stanza. This can be a simple statement or question, such as *Do you think we'll find a way of living together?* There should be space for every living thing in the habitat. The group can assign a member to write and illustrate a clean copy of this stanza.

Ask groups to read their poems aloud to the class. Three group members can take turns reading the three stanzas and showing the accompanying pictures. Or the whole group can practice and present a choral reading of the entire poem, with each member reading his or her lines in the first two stanzas and the whole group reading the final stanza together.

Conclude the activity by discussing the word pictures in the poems and how they make the listeners feel. Make copies of the poems for children to take home. Invite students to think of and carry out ways to share their poems with other classes.

SOCIAL STUDIES: WHAT DID IT USED TO BE LIKE?

Challenge interested students working at a Grade 3 level to team up with partners and do research to find out what plants and animals flourished in your area before it was heavily settled. Suggest students use local libraries, local historical societies, and museums to do their research. Your researchers can report their findings via a mural or by writing and illustrating a book, using *Heron Street* as a model.

APPLYING THE SCIENCE CONCEPT:

Invite students to periodically report news—gleaned from radio, TV, or newspapers—about human activities in your area that are destroying, rebuilding, or maintaining the natural habitats of animals and plants. Where practical, ask students how they can get involved in helping to preserve the natural habitats.

From *Science & Stories, Grades K-3*, published by GoodYearBooks. Copyright © 1994 Hilarie N. Staton and Tara McCarthy.

Heron Street

Name _____ Date _____

MY FIELD TRIP RECORD

DIRECTIONS

Draw a picture to go with each caption.

A leaf with smooth edges or deeply-cut edges	A leaf with notches
A plant that is green	A plant that is red, pink, orange, brown, yellow, white, or purple
Something that is soft, fluffy, or hairy	Something that is hard or bumpy
An insect and where it was resting or moving	A bird and what it was doing

What other animals did you see? Draw pictures of them on the other side of this record or on a separate sheet of paper.

LITERATURE:
Miss Rumphius
Barbara Cooney (Puffin Books, 1982)

SCIENCE:
Patterns of Change

UNDERSTANDING:
Humans have the responsibility to use earth's resources wisely.

INQUIRY SKILLS:
Observing, predicting, inferring, manipulating materials, identifying variables

From *Science & Stories*, Grades K-3, published by GoodYearBooks. Copyright © 1994 Hilarie N. Staton and Tara McCarthy.

AHEAD (of) TIME

WHAT YOU'LL NEED

For Building the Science Connection
- variety of children's nature periodicals (see the Bibliography on page 129)
- writing and art materials
- scratch paper

For Follow-Up Activities
- cassette tape recorder with internal or external microphone and blank cassette tape (Oral Language)
- art materials for making books—construction paper, colored pencils or crayons, scissors, glue, paper punch, yarn or brads for binding pages (Writing)

STORY SUMMARY

The narrator tells about her aging aunt, Alice Rumphius, known in the community as the Lupine Lady. When Alice was a little girl, she told her seafaring father her two wishes: that she would travel to faraway lands, and that she would live in a place by the sea. Her father approved of these wishes, but added a stricture: "You must do something to make the world more beautiful." As she grows up, Miss Rumphius acts out her first wish and travels to many lands. As she grows old, Miss Rumphius has her second wish come true: she lives in a house by the sea. But how can she carry out her father's advice to make the world more beautiful? Miss Rumphius does this by planting lupine (LOO-pin) seeds along the paths and roads of her town, and in the fields and on the hills. Now each year the purple, blue, and rose-colored lupines festoon the town with beauty. And the narrator, Miss Rumphius's niece, wonders how she, too, might make the world more beautiful.

READING STRATEGIES

PRE-READING

After showing the book cover and reading the title, explain that the story is about a woman who has three wishes or hopes about what she wants to do in the world. All her wishes come true, and the cover picture gives a hint as to what one of them is. Encourage students to guess this wish and write their predictions on the chalkboard. Brainstorm another list of what the other two wishes might be. Then invite students to listen to the story to check their predictions about Miss Rumphius.

WHILE READING

Before reading each page in the first half of the story, invite students to examine the accompanying illustrations to find clues about where and when the action is taking place. This predicting strategy will build students' sense of the time span covered in the story (many decades), of the gradual aging of the heroine, and of the fact that she is making her own wishes come true. After finishing the page that begins "From the porch of her new house. . .," ask students what they think Miss Rumphius will do to make the world more beautiful. Then read the story to the end. When you finish the story, go back to the Pre-Reading predictions that the students made and discuss the predictions in light of what they've found out about Miss Rumphius. Save the list for use in the Follow-Up Writing activity.

SCIENCE STRATEGIES
BUILDING THE SCIENCE CONNECTION

Invite students to work in groups of six or eight to develop practical ways that they, as children, can help make the world more beautiful or care for its resources. Introduce the activity by reviewing what Miss Rumphius did in this regard and how her niece now wants to make the world more beautiful too. To point out that young people actually can make such contributions, share this good news with your class:

Children in Guilderland, New York, planted lupine seeds, too, in wild, protected areas. They did this as a way of saving a tiny butterfly called the Karner blue. The butterfly is extremely rare, and was on the verge of extinction, for it will eat and lay its eggs on only one kind of flower, the lupine. Fields of lupine have been destroyed as people build houses, shopping malls, and roads. The children got a scientist to show them how to collect lupine seeds and how to plant them. Now the lupines are blooming in many places again, and the children hope the Karner blues will find their new homes and make a comeback.

Put the children's periodicals in a central location. Explain that each group will choose several periodicals and study them to help get ideas about (a) environmental problems that need to be solved; and (b) possible ways of solving them (stress that these periodicals are for getting ideas). Some of the problems mentioned in them are special to faraway places. Some of the problems are so big that teams of experts are needed to solve them.

Groups should look for the kinds of problems for which they could realistically develop solutions, as the children in Guilderland did. Some of your students may already be aware of local environmental problems that need attention.

Suggest they look through the periodicals to find stories about similar problems and solutions. After groups have chosen their periodicals, distribute Activity Sheet 24. Review with the class the three questions that each group will eventually answer.

Suggest the following procedure and roles: Partners within the group will independently go through three or four of the magazines and use scrap paper as bookmarks to mark ideas to discuss with the group as a whole. The whole group will then discuss the different ideas and decide on the one that suggests a project they could carry out.

Group members discuss together how to answer each question on the Activity Sheet. A group scribe can write a draft of each answer on scrap paper, an editor can revise and edit it, and three group members can copy the final draft onto the Activity Sheet. One or two members can draw illustrations on separate sheets of paper to illustrate each answer.

After groups have shared and discussed their work with the class, compile the Activity Sheets and illustrations in a folder for your classroom science center. The natural outcome of this activity is that many of your students will want to implement one or more of the suggestions in the folder. They can begin to do this in Extending the Science Connection.

EXTENDING THE SCIENCE CONNECTION
List the groups' different proposed projects on the chalkboard. Praise the good points about each. Guide a class discussion about general feasibility (Do we have room? Do we have time? Can we find family members, community people, and experts to help us?) Your input is important here! Then have students vote for the project they would like to try first. Ask volunteers to help you contact by letter the resource people you will need to make the project work. Since most such projects will take extended periods of time to accomplish, keep interest and motivation high by linking the project to the rest of your curriculum whenever possible, as with the following activities.

FOLLOW-UP ACTIVITIES
ORAL LANGUAGE: BOOK-PEOPLE INTERVIEWS
This activity will help students develop questioning strategies they'll need as they work with the outside people who'll help with the class project. Invite partners to choose a book they've enjoyed in which a character helps to solve a problem or shares special facts. One partner will play the part of the character, and the other will be the interviewer. For example, an interviewer can ask Miss Rumphius how to plant lupines. Examples of other books from Science and Literature Connections that can be used this way are (a)*Witch Hazel.* The interviewer can ask questions about growing pumpkins, and the character, Johnny, can answer them; (b) *Owl Moon.* The interviewer can ask Pa or the child questions about what

kind of habitat an owl needs in order to survive; and (c) *Heron Street.* The interviewer can ask the heron or a wolf why it left the marsh and what might be done to restore its habitat.

Provide time for your acting duos to practice their interviews before they present them to the class. If possible, tape record the final versions. Make the tapes available in your reading center for students to enjoy and discuss independently.

WRITING: WISH BOOKS
Invite students to work independently or with partners to write and illustrate a *Three Wishes Book.* Introduce the activity by reviewing the three wishes Miss Rumphius has: to travel, to live by the sea, and to make the world more beautiful. Suggest that students make their first two wishes experiences or adventures that they want for themselves. (You might do some preliminary brainstorming here to encourage students to wish, as Miss Rumphius does, for experiences rather than for material objects.) Explain that the last wish might be for one thing or action that will help restore or preserve some natural phenomenon, e.g., a particular animal or plant, or some wild landform like a canyon, cave, swift river, or wide seashore.

After students read and show their "Wish Books" to classmates, find a way to publish them for wider circulation. You might have them typed up and copied for circulation to other classrooms and for taking home. If your local newspaper encourages submissions from schools, having your students' wishes printed for wide circulation can help raise community awareness about children's concerns, and also be a source of pride and motivation for your budding writers.

SOCIAL STUDIES: EVALUATING CHANGES
✓ Whatever your social studies program, it will deal with change. Encourage students to identify changes and evaluate their effects on

From *Science & Stories*, Grades K-3, published by GoodYearBooks. Copyright © 1994 Hilarie N. Staton and Tara McCarthy.

the environment. Which changes do they think make life better for humans? for other living things? Which changes bring problems to solve? Allow for wide-ranging discussions that encourage a variety of thoughts and opinions. Invite interested students to make charts, diagrams, or other visual organizers that show how a change affects different people and different natural resources in different ways.

CIVICS: KEEPING UP WITH NEWS ABOUT THE ENVIRONMENT

Encourage your students to listen to national and local TV and radio programs to identify current environmental problems and issues. What is the problem? What solutions are being suggested? Invite interested students to form an "Environmental Watchdog Committee." The committee should report to the class periodically about environmental issues that committee members have heard discussed via the media.

FUNCTIONAL WRITING: LETTERS

As a spinoff from the activity above, encourage students to write letters to people, groups, or corporations who are influential in environmental issues. Letters can be thank-you notes to people who have made decisions the writer approves of, or opinion letters to people who are in the process of making policy, or disapproving letters to people or groups who have enacted policies that a student thinks are harmful to the environment. To help make sure the letters get sent, secure a compendium like *America's Phone Book* (ARCO), which lists the addresses and phone numbers of major corporations and government agencies.

APPLYING THE SCIENCE CONCEPT:

To help children realize that small, thoughtful actions add up to a lot, post a class "Miss Rumphius's Helping-the-World-Today Record" on your bulletin board. Invite students to log-in daily entries that show their concern for the environment. Examples are: "I helped separate things that will be recycled." "I picked up the litter along the side of my lawn." "I got my family to call the ASPCA about a sick raccoon we saw in the backyard." "I made a bird feeder to help birds make it through the winter." "I taught my little brother how to turn off the water faucet so he wouldn't waste water."

Miss Rumphius

Name _____ Date _____

A PROBLEM TO SOLVE

DIRECTIONS
Follow the directions your teacher gives you.

1. What is the problem?

_____

_____

_____

2. What caused the problem?

_____

_____

_____

3. What is something we can do to help solve the problem?

_____

_____

_____

_____

From *Science & Stories*, Grades K-3, published by GoodYearBooks. Copyright © 1994 Hilarie N. Staton and Tara McCarthy.

Resources

MORE RECOMMENDED LITERATURE

The titles are listed in conjunction with titles featured in *Science & Stories*. This arrangement provides you easy access to additional books that can further help develop the specific science understanding or skill in the lesson. Starred titles denote books that are related to the literary theme in the story.

STORY 1 *WITCH HAZEL*

Gibbons, Gail. *From Seed to Plant.* (Holiday House, 1992).

Jordan, Helene J. *How a Seed Grows.* (HarperCollins, 1992).

Luenn, Nancy. *Mother Earth.* (Atheneum, 1992).

Markmann, Erika. *Grow It! An Indoor/Outdoor Gardening Guide for Kids.* (Random House, 1991).

*McKissak, Patricia. *A Million Fish . . . More or Less.* (Knopf, 1992).

STORY 2 *WHISTLE FOR WILLIE*

Aliki. *At Mary Bloom's.* (Greenwillow, 1983).

Allen, Pamela. *Bertie and the Bear.* (Coward, 1984).

Aylesworth, Jim. *Country Crossing.* (Atheneum, 1991).

Brown, Margaret Wise. *The Quiet Noisy Book.* (HarperCollins, 1993).

Carle, Eric. *The Very Busy Spider.* (Philomel, 1984).

Dobbs, Dayle Ann. *Wheel Away!* (Harper & Row, 1989).

STORY 3 *OWL MOON*

Banks, Mary. *Animals of the Night.* (Scribner's, 1990).

Greenaway, F. *Amazing Bats.* (Knopf, 1991).

McDonald, M. *"Whoo-oo Is It?"* (Orchard, 1992).

Mowat, Farley. *Owls in the Family.* (Bantam, 1985).

*San Souci, Daniel. *North Country Night.* (Doubleday, 1990).

Savage, Stephen. *Making Tracks.* (Lodestar, 1992).

STORY 4 *I WONDER IF I'LL SEE A WHALE*

The Cousteau Society Series: Seals; Dolphins; Penguins; Turtles. (Simon and Schuster, 1992).

Gibbons, Gail. *Sharks.* (Holiday, 1992).

Jacobs, Francine. *Sam the Sea Cow.* (Walker, 1992).

McMillan, B. *Going on a Whale Watch.* (Scholastic, 1992).

*Ryder, J. *Winter Whale.* (Morrow, 1991).

STORY 5 *TIGER*

Chinery, Michael. *Tell Me About Series: Desert Animals; Grassland Animals; Ocean Animals; Rainforest Animals.* (Random House, 1991).

*Cowcher, Helen. *Tigress.* (Farrar, Straus, 1991).

Hirschi, R. *Where Do Cats Live?* (Walker, 1991).

Lewin, Ted. *Tiger Trek.* (Macmillan, 1990).

Raffi. *The Raffi Singable Song Book.* (Crown, 1987).

Urquhart, J. C. *Lions and Tigers and Leopards: The Big Cats.* (National Geographic Society, 1990).

Whipple, Laura. *Eric Carle's Animals, Animals.* (Philomel, 1989).

STORY 6 *ALEXANDER AND THE WIND-UP MOUSE*

* Andersen, H. C. *The Nightingale,* translated by Eva Le Gallienne. (Harper & Row, 1965).

Miller, Edna. *Mousekin's Birth.* (Prentice-Hall, 1974).

White, E. B. *Stuart Little.* (Harper & Row, 1945).

STORY 7 *THE VERY HUNGRY CATERPILLAR*

Schoenherr, John. *Bear.* (Philomel, 1991).

Stevenson, James. *Which One Is Whitney?* (Greenwillow, 1990).

Watts, Barrie. *See How They Grow Series: Rabbit; Kitten; Puppy; Duck; Frog; Chick.* (Lodestar, Dutton, 1991).

STORY 8 *THE MIXED-UP CHAMELEON*

Baker, Keith. *Hide and Snake.* (Harcourt, 1991).

Carle, Eric. *Do You Want to Be My Friend?* (Harper & Row, 1987).

Guiberson, Brenda. *Cactus Hotel.* (Holt, 1991).

*Mazer, A. *The Salamander Room.* (Knopf, 1991).

Sowler, Sandie. *Amazing Animal Disguises.* (Knopf, 1992).

STORY 9 *OX-CART MAN*

Cholene, Terri. *Dancing Drum: A Cherokee Legend.* (Troll Assoc., 1990).

*Fraser, Debra. *On the Day You Were Born.* (Harcourt, 1991).

Llewellyn, Claire. *My First Book of Time.* (Dorling, 1992).

Maestro, Betsy. *Let's Read and Find Out About Science: How Do Apples Grow?* (Harper, 1992).

Micucci, Charles. *The Life and Times of the Apple.* (Orchard, 1992).

*Paladino, Catherine. *Spring Fleece: A Day of Sheep-Shearing.* (Joy Street, 1990).

STORY 10 *THE LEGEND OF THE BLUEBONNET*

*Goble, Paul. *Dream Wolf.* (Bradbury, 1991).

Jeunesse, G., and De Bourgoing, P., *Weather.* (Scholastic, 1989).

Sewall, Marcia. *People of the Breaking Day.* (Atheneum, 1990).

STORY 11 *TIME OF WONDER*

Berger, Melvin. *Seasons.* (Doubleday, 1990).

Carlstorm, N. W. *Goodbye Geese.* (Philomel, 1991).

*Weisner, David. *Hurricane.* (Clarion, 1991).

STORY 12 *THE NIGHTGOWN OF THE SULLEN MOON*

Barrett, Norman S. *A Picture World of Astronauts; Planets; Space Voyages; Sun and Stars.* (Franklin Watts, 1990).

*Greenfield, Eloise. *Night on Neighborhood Street.* (Dial, 1991).

Kitamura, Satoshi. *UFO Diary.* (Farrar Straus Giroux, 1989).

*Ryder, Joanne. *The Bear on the Moon.* (Morrow, 1991).

Thurber, James. *Many Moons.* (Harcourt, 1990).

From *Science & Stories,* Grades K-3, published by GoodYearBooks. Copyright © 1994 Hilarie N. Staton and Tara McCarthy.

STORY 13 *KATY AND THE BIG SNOW*

Berger, Fredericka. *Robots: What They Are, What They Do.* (Greenwillow, 1992).

Kerrod, Robin. *Amazing Flying Machines.* (Knopf, 1992).

Lord, Trevor. *Amazing Cars.* (Knopf, 1992).

Taylor, Kim. *Flying Start Science Series: Water; Light; Action; Structure.* (Wiley, 1992).

STORY 14 *THE MAGIC FAN*

Ishii, Mamokoto. *The Tongue-Cut Sparrow.* (Lodestar, 1987).

Jones, Ann. *Reflections.* (Greenwillow, 1987).

*LaMorisse, Albert. *The Red Balloon.* (Doubleday, 1956).

Marshak, Suzanna. *I Am the Ocean.* (Arcade/Little, Brown, 1991).

Matsumo, Masako. *A Pair of Red Clogs.* (World, 1960).

Newton, Montgomery. *The Five Sparrows: A Japanese Folktale.* (Atheneum, 1982).

Peters, Lisa. *The Sun, the Wind, and the Rain.* (Henry Holt, 1988).

Robbins, Ken. *Beach Days.* (Viking, 1987).

Zion, Gene. *Harry by the Sea.* (Harper & Row, 1965).

STORY 15 *HOW TO DIG A HOLE TO THE OTHER SIDE OF THE WORLD*

Cole, Joanna. *The Magic School Bus Inside the Earth.* (Scholastic, 1987).

Ester, Alison. *The Journey Home.* (Houghton, 1991).

Ryder, Joanne. *Under Your Feet.* (Four Winds, 1991).

Schleir, M. *Let's Go Dinosaur Tracking.* (HarperCollins, 1991).

STORY 16 *HILL OF FIRE*

*DePaola, Tomie. *The Prince of the Dolomites.* (Harcourt, 1980).

Siebert, Diane. *Sierra.* (HarperCollins, 1991).

STORY 17 *GREGORY, THE TERRIBLE EATER*

*Barrett, Judi. *Cloudy with a Chance of Meatballs.* (Atheneum, 1978).

Parnell, Peter. *Woodpile.* (Macmillan, 1990).

STORY 18 *BRINGING THE RAIN TO KAPITI PLAIN*

Butterfield, N. *Flower.* (Simon & Schuster, 1991).

Myers, Christopher and Myers, Lynne Born. *McCrephy's Field.* (Houghton, 1991).

Royston, Angela. *What's Inside?: Plants.* (Dorling, 1992).

Weir, Bob and Weir, Wendy. *Panther Dream: A Story of the African Rainforest.* (Little, Brown, 1991).

STORY 19 *THE STORY OF JUMPING MOUSE*

*Hong, Lily Toy. *How the Ox Star Fell from Heaven.* (Albert Whitman, 1991).

*Mollel, Tololwa. *The Orphan Boy.* (Clarion, 1991).

Tresselt, Alvin. *The Gift of the Tree.* (Lothrop, 1992).

STORY 20 *MANDY*

Aseltine, L. and Mueller, E. *I'm Deaf and It's Okay.* (Albert Whitman, 1986).

Cox, James. *Put Your Foot in Your Mouth and Other Silly Sayings.* (Random House, 1988).

Dwight, Laura. *We Can Do It!* (Checkerboard, 1992).

Guccione, L. *Tell Me How the Wind Sounds.*
(Scholastic, 1989).

Gwynne, Fred. *A Chocolate Moose for Dinner.*
(Simon and Schuster, 1988).

Nevins, Ann. *From the Horse's Mouth.*
(Prentice-Hall, 1977).

Parish, Peggy. *Amelia Bedelia.*
(Harper & Row, 1963).

Isking, M. *Apple Is My Sign.*
(Houghton Mifflin, 1981).

STORY 21 *THE MAGIC SCHOOL BUS INSIDE THE HUMAN BODY*
Aliki. *I'm Growing!* (HarperCollins, 1992).

Cumbaa, Stephen. *The Bones Book and Skeleton.*
(Workman, 1991).

Machotka, H. *Breathtaking Noses.*
(Morrow, 1992).

Rockwell, Robert E. and Williams, Robert A.
Everybody Has a Body: Science from Head to Toe.
(Gryphon, 1992).

STORY 22 *LETTING SWIFT RIVER GO*
*Baker, Jeannie. *Window.* (Greenwillow, 1991).

Cole, Joanna. *The Magic School Bus at the Waterworks.* (Scholastic, 1988).

*Locker, Thomas. *Where the River Begins.*
(Dial, 1984).

STORY 23 *HERON STREET*
Bash, Barbara. *Urban Roosts: Where Birds Nest in the City.* (Sierra Club/Little, Brown, 1990).

Cherry, Lynne. *The Great Kapok Tree: A Tale of the Amazon Rain Forest.* (Harcourt, 1990).

Guiberson, Brenda Z. *Spoonbill Swamp.*
(Holt, 1992).

Milton, Joyce. *Wild, Wild Wolves.*
(Random House, 1992).

Rockwell, Anne. *Our Yard Is Full of Birds.*
(Macmillan, 1992).

STORY 24 *MISS RUMPHIUS*
*George, William T. *Fishing at Long Pond.*
(Greenwillow, 1991).

Gibbons, Gail. *Recycle! A Handbook for Kids.*
(Little, Brown, 1992).

*Lewis, J. Patrick. *Earth Verses and Water Rhymes.*
(Atheneum, 1991).

PROFESSIONAL BOOKS AND PERIODICALS

Allman, A. S. and Koop, O. W. *Environmental Education: Guideline Activities for Children and Youth* (Merrill, 1976).

Baker, Dave, Sample, Cheryl, and Stead, Tony.
How Big Is the Moon? Whole Math in Action
(Heinemann, 1990).

Bowden, Marcia. *Nature for the Very Young: A Handbook of Indoor and Outdoor Activities*
(Wiley, 1989).

Caduto, Michael J. and Bruchac, Joseph. *Keepers of the Earth* (Fulcrum, 1989).

Driver, R. and Guesne, E. *Children's Ideas in Science* (Open University Press, 1985).

Farndon, John. *How the Earth Works: 100 Ways Parents and Kids Can Share the Secrets of the Earth* (Reader's Digest, 1992).

Lingelbach, Jenepher, ed. *Hands-on Nature: Information and Activities for Exploring the Environment with Children*
(Vermont Institute of Natural Science, 1986).

Moutran, Julia Spencer. *Elementary Science Activities for All Seasons* (Simon & Schuster, 1990).

Project Wild and Project Aquatic
Western Regional Environmental Council, P. O.
Box 18060, Boulder, CO 80308-8060.

From *Science & Stories, Grades K–3*, published by GoodYearBooks. Copyright © 1994 Hilarie N. Staton and Tara McCarthy.

Richardson, Elwyn. *In the Early World* (New Zealand Council for Educational Research, 1964).

Russell, Helen Ross. *Ten-Minute Field Trips* (Ferguson, 1973).

Schmidt, V. and Rockcastle, V. *Teaching Science with Everyday Things* (McGraw-Hill, 1968).

Science and Children, (published eight times a year National Science Teachers Association, Washington, DC).

Sisson, Edith. *Nature with Children of All Ages: Activities and Adventures for Exploring, Learning, and Enjoying the World Around Us* (Prentice-Hall, 1982).

Tant, Carl. *Projects: Making Hands-on Science Easy, a Guide to Science Project Management with Stress Prevention for Teachers and Parents* (Biotech, 1992).

Water, Precious Water: Project AIMS; A Collection of Elementary Water Activities (AIMS Education Foundation, P. O. Box 776, Fresno, CA 93747).

SOFTWARE

Bank Street School Filer. Apple IIe and IIgs; Commodore 64. Students practice classifying by creating an "animal data base." (Sunburst Communications, 101 Castleton Street, Pleasantville, NY 10570)

Mammals: A Multimedia Encyclopedia. IBM PS/2 or compatible with 640K, CD ROM drive, VGA color monitor. This is an exciting way to learn, for kindergartners as well as sixth-graders. (National Geographic Society, 17th and M Streets N.W., Washington, DC 20036)

Muppet Labs. Apple II and IIgs with 128K. Working with objects and concepts from science, Grade K–1 students learn matching, sorting, classifying, reasoning, and observing skills. (Sunburst Communications, 101 Castleton Street, Pleasantville, NY 10570)

Science Explorers: Vol. 1 Plant Explorer, Weather Explorer, Shadows, Skeleton Explorer. Apple, IBM, or MS-DOS. Four double-sided disks, back-up labels, and an 82-page manual. (Scholastic, Inc., 730 Broadway, New York, NY 10003)

OTHER MULTIMEDIA MATERIALS

Coronet Films and Video, 108 Wilmot Road, Deerfield, IL 60015.

Encyclopedia Brittanica Education Corporation, 425 N. Michigan Avenue, Chicago, IL 60611.

Random House Media, Dept. 451, 400 Hahn Road, Westminster, MD 21157.

Schoolmasters Science and Teaching Aids, Dept. 88A, 745 State Circle, P. O. Box 1941, Ann Arbor, MI 48106.

Troll Associates, 320 Route 17, Mahwah, NJ 07430.

PERIODICALS FOR STUDENTS

Dolphin Log. The Cousteau Society, 930 West 21 Street, Norfolk, VA 23517.

National Geographic World. National Geographic World, P. O. Box 2330, Washington, DC 20077-9955.

Owl Magazine. P. O. Box 11314, Des Moines, IA 50340.

Ranger Rick. National Wildlife Federation, 8925 Leesburg Pike, Vienna, VA 22180-0001.

Zoobooks. Wildlife Education, Ltd., 3590 Kettner Boulevard, San Diego, CA 92101.